EFL UNIT, DEPT. LANG & LING
UNIVERSITY OF ESSEX
COLCHESTER CO4 3SQ
GREAT BRITAIN

Published by The British Council
ISBN 0 86355 237 4

Designed and typeset by The British Council
Printed in Britain by Thornton and Pearson Ltd

The British Council is registered in England as a charity no. 209131

Britain in view

BBC Newsroom South-East

Notes for teachers: ways of exploiting the material

This book has been written to accompany the video, Britain in view, which consists of fifteen news clips recorded from BBC Newsroom South-East during the early 1990s. Each clip has been chosen because it features an aspect of life in contemporary Britain likely to be of interest to learners and teachers of English.

The book is intended to provide help in working with the video clips and the supporting newspaper and magazine articles, although the articles themselves and the British Studies sections could be used independently of the video cassette.

All the source material is 'authentic', that is to say the video clips and extracts from the national press and other articles were written for a British audience and have not been adapted in any way for English language teaching. The material is suitable for learners of intermediate level upwards, and the transcripts and units in this book have been provided to help learners and their teachers understand and enjoy the source material.

Using the video

The background notes set the clip in context and explain difficult words and references, and the pre-viewing section then helps learners focus their attention on and make predictions about what is to follow. The video should always be played through a first time for general comprehension. The comprehension questions have been ordered in such a way that they refer to consecutive parts of the video, so that the relevant sections can be replayed in turn. The students should read the questions they have to answer before viewing the relevant part. In this way they know what to listen out for and are not side-tracked by other bits of information. If they made predictions about the content, these can be checked to see if they were right.

The number of times the video or various sections of it are replayed will vary according to how it is used. It can be played and replayed for more intensive listening such as listening out for any numbers that were used and asking which bits of the video they occurred in, and what they referred to. It can also be used for picking out exact words that were used. The students should always have access to the transcript for the final viewing so that any difficulties in understanding can be cleared up. The transcripts, which are to be found at the end of the book, will be needed for the exercises.

It is possible also to exploit the video for both sound and image separately. For instance, the group can be divided into pairs with one from each pair listening to a cassette of the sound recording, and the other watching the images without sound. The listener tries to write down as much of the commentary as possible, and the viewer constructs a story out of what can be seen. The cassette should be played through twice, and the pairs then meet up to reconstruct the real story.

To exploit the pictures alone, the sound should be turned down and each member of the group should construct his or her own version of what is happening. The video should be played through twice, so that the first time through the students can simply make a list of the various scenes that they see. During the second viewing they can then fill in more details. Versions can be compared firstly with each other, and later with the original.

The articles

These have been chosen to supplement the video by presenting the same issue from a different angle, or a related issue arising from or connected with the theme of the video clip. They have been selected from newspapers, journals and magazines from the 'quality' press and specialist publications, in order to provide a variety of different styles of writing. If desired, they may be used separately from the video for both linguistic and stylistic purposes. They also provide useful material for students to practise reading aloud.

Activities

1 Comprehension

This section takes the form of either direct questions, gap-filling exercises, true/false statements, or asking for a summary. Where it is divided into two parts, the first part relates to overall comprehension, and the second to a more detailed understanding of the video/article.

2 Language focus

The first element in this section requires a piece of written work by the student. This can take the form of a letter, a summary, a report, a brief article, or a personal opinion, where the student is invited to adopt a particular point of view or a particular style, and to use the grammar and vocabulary appropriate to that view or style. The student may be asked to decide which linguistic features are appropriate to a particular style.

The rest of the section draws attention to stylistic features found in the video clip or the article. The purpose of this is to show how language is manipulated to serve different linguistic ends, e.g. one of the uses of the passive is to make things more formal and less personal. The video material provides a variety of spoken styles, and the articles a variety of written styles. This will help the student learn to recognize the linguistic markers appropriate to different styles of speaking and writing.

Many of the tasks required of the student in this section can be developed in more detail by the teacher in the classroom, or they can be worked on by students working in a self-access centre.

3 Oral focus

This section contains points for discussion or role plays, or invites learners to express personal opinions or attitudes. Activities are based on the topics and ideas occurring in or arising from the video clips and articles, and are designed to promote both individual self-expression and group discussion.

***British Studies* section**

This section considers some of the aspects of British life presented in the video clips. This is done with the presentation of a set of statistics or some factual information relating to a particular topic. Questions have been designed to be answered in the classroom either orally or in writing, with students working individually or as a group on the information provided. There then follows a project to be undertaken as a group activity outside the classroom. In this way, students will be encouraged to find out what happens in their own country with regard to certain areas of national interest, and then compare that with what happens in Britain. The tasks have been designed so that each member of the class/group can be involved in the activities, e.g. preparing questionnaires and asking people to fill them in, interviewing people, analyzing the information gained, and then producing the final statistics, tables, or report.

For the purposes of this section, it has been assumed that the classes will be monolingual. Where, however the classes are multilingual, previous experience has shown that such tasks can be adapted on an individual basis.

Anne Dyson
Oxford
November 1993

Flower thieves

Background

National Environment Week is a week set aside for highlighting and promoting environmental issues.

Garden centres have become very fashionable over the last ten to fifteen years, and cater for the gardener's every need. As well as selling seeds and plants, they sell gardening tools, garden furniture and even conservatories. They have become big business in the leisure industry, and many people visit them for a family day out.

A nursery in this context is a place where plants are grown for sale.

Note: Sphagnum moss is very popular with gardeners and its water retention properties make it especially useful for lining hanging baskets.

Pre-viewing

Focusing on **why, where,** and **what**

Why do you think people would want to steal flowers?

Where would they steal them from?

What would they do with them when they had stolen them?

Video

A The main issue

What is worrying conservationists in Oxfordshire and the south-east?

More detail

1 Which plant is being protected in the Chiltern Hills?

2 How is it protected by law?

3 Describe how the conservationists are trying to protect it?

4 What damage is caused if the flowering plant is stolen?

5 What other plants are under attack?

6 Why are the plants being stolen?

7 What additional law do the conservationists propose?

B Language focus

It takes all sorts ...

There is a conflict of interest between the parties mentioned in the video report, with conservationists and wardens opposed to collectors and gangs of thieves. Write a brief account (eighty words) of the situation from the conservationists' point of view attacking opposing groups. You might find it helpful to use expressions such as:

'clearly pointless'
'motivated by greed'
'plundering the nature reserves'

The irony of the situation

What phrase is used to express the increasing interest in environmental concerns? Explain in about fifty words, how this could have contributed to the problem described in the video.

What do you think?

(a) There seems to be a ready market for the pickings.
(b) There seems to be no difficulty in selling what they have taken.

Why do you think the reporter said (a) rather than (b)?

Can you suggest a suitable context for (b)?

(c) Organized crime is plundering the nature reserves.

What kind of activity is suggested by the verb 'plunder'? What context would you usually expect it to appear in? What is the effect of its use here?

(d) One of the speakers contrasts 'large reputable garden centres' with 'smaller backstreet nurseries'.

What is he implying by the use of the word 'backstreet'? Does 'smaller' suggest anything other than size?

And so on and so forth ...

In paragraph 7 the speaker finishes his first sentence with 'and so on', and his second one with 'and so on and so forth'. These expressions are very common in everyday speech. Can you suggest what purpose they serve?

C Role play

You are a conservationist. Explain why you think it necessary to have tighter laws to protect plants, and say what further measures you would take against flower thieves.

Discussion

In pairs, discuss the ways in which you personally have become more environmentally aware. Do you, for example, do any of the following:

- recycle bottles and newspapers (are there any collection points near where you live?)
- use unleaded petrol?
- buy 'green' products?
- cycle or travel by public transport?

As a group, share your findings and see if you have any concerns in common. Then suggest possible further courses of action you might take, either as individuals or as a group.

Return of the native at ground level

Della Denman visits the orchid unit at Kew, a safe haven for the rare European species

One of the best-kept secrets in British horticultural circles is the whereabouts of the last surviving Lady's Slipper Orchid. Only one specimen remains, closely guarded day and night during the flowering season in a remote hillside site somewhere in England.

No other clue can be disclosed because experts fear for its safety. The Lady's Slipper, our largest and most glamorous orchid, was so widely picked, pressed and collected by the Victorians that it was thought extinct at the turn of the century. The surviving plant was discovered in the 1930s.

The propagation of rare and endangered wild orchids is the concern of an intriguing conservation unit established at the Royal Botanic Gardens, Kew, in 1983. It is run by Joyce Stewart, an orchid specialist who is investigating 50 rare British species and 100 even rarer European types. The unit, a joint project between Kew and English Nature, was sponsored by Sir Robert and Lady Sainsbury, who gave their own tropical orchid collection to Kew in the early 1980s. When they realised that many temperate British natives were in danger of becoming extinct, they made a £1 million endowment to Kew to fund a research project.

Joyce Stewart at Kew

Sandwiched between Kew's laboratories on the outskirts of the public garden is a greenhouse filled with dozens of pots of tiny orchid seedlings, all raised from seed. At this time of year, Mrs Stewart and her research assistants wait and watch in anticipation to see if they will flower and set seed. Another glasshouse shimmers in a haze of pinks, purples and yellows. These are the flowers of mature orchids from all over Europe that have been successfully grown at Kew over the past few years.

The orchid's mystique comes from its beautiful colour and shape, its scent, and in many cases its rarity. It is one of the most highly evolved of all plants. And its distinctive "lip", which often provides a landing platform for the pollinating insect, can be shaped like a pouch, horn, tail, ruffle or fringe. There are around 25,000 different species, and more man-made hybrids are recorded every year. Yet the rarest appear in only a few known colonies. Ten of our 50 British species are protected because they are found in only two of three sites. It is illegal to pick or uproot them.

The Daily Telegraph – 18 April 1992

Return of the native at ground level

A True or false?

1 There are several specimens of the Lady's Slipper Orchid.

2 The Orchid Unit was sponsored by Lord and Lady Sainsbury.

3 The Victorians never collected orchids.

4 The orchid is one of the most highly evolved of all plants.

5 Fifty British species of orchid are protected.

B Language focus

Summary

Summarize the history and purpose of the Orchid Unit at Kew in four sentences basing each sentence on one of the following key words used in any order:

- propagation, sponsored, investigating, endowment

What purpose does it serve?

Paragraph 2 of the article consists of three sentences written in the passive voice. Rewrite sentence 2 in the active, and suggest reasons why it, and sentence 3 were originally written in the passive.

Find the original expression

Replace the words or phrases in bold with the words or phrases used in the article:

(a) Many species of British orchids were in danger of **dying out**. (paragraph 3)
(b) It is **against the law** to pick the rare orchids. (paragraph 5)
(c) There is a **sense of the mysterious and the unusual** about orchids. (paragraph 5)
(d) The orchid is one of the most **highly developed** of plants. (paragraph 5)
(e) The greenhouse is **squeezed in tightly** between the laboratories. (paragraph 4)

Keeping it secret

The first two paragraphs of the article use the following expressions:

- best-kept secrets, last surviving, closely guarded day and night, remote hillside, clue, disclosed, fear, safety

In what kind of writing would you usually expect to find such words and expressions? What is the effect on the reader of their use here?

C Discussion

If you had £1 million to spend on a conservation project, which one would you choose? Would you want to preserve flowers, animals, or birds?

Gardening is a very popular leisure activity, but many people don't have a garden. Suggest the advantages of having one from a leisure, a health, and an economic point of view.

If you could grow only one flower, which would it be? Give reasons for your choice.

Salmon return to the Thames

Background

The National Rivers Authority (NRA) was established by the 1989 Water Act and is a major environmental protection agency. It is responsible for safeguarding and improving the natural water environment.

Thames Water, now a privatized water company, was responsible for the River Thames before the NRA was created.

Pre-viewing

What is implied by the word 'return' in the title of the clip?

Can you think of any reasons why the salmon might have left?

Suggest a reason why their return has been brought to our attention in the video report.

Video

A The issues

1 State the purpose of the NRA's salmon programme.

2 Explain why salmon are regarded as good indicators of water quality.

What happened when?

Put the following dates and expressions of time in the order in which they occur in the extract, and say what they refer to:

- two hundred years ago, 1834, centuries ago, 1974, 1979, today

B Language focus

State your case

You are an environmentalist who has been asked to write a brief account of your views about the NRA's salmon programme. As you are very impressed, write a very positive account comparing the present situation with the very poor situation which preceded it. Which of the following linguistic features might you use?

- **making statements**
  adjectives
  negatives

- **asking questions**
  adverbs of manner
  superlatives

- **making demands**
  adverbs of place
  exclamations

The things people say

Read paragraph 3 of the transcript and pick out two linguistic features that indicate that this was originally a spoken text.

Rewrite the paragraph as a written text.

Putting on a good face

Pick out the phrases used in the text that express the same ideas as those written in bold in the sentences below:

(a) The NRA **want to improve their reputation with the public** in the area of pollution. (paragraph 2)

(b) The environmentalist's view is that the NRA's action is a **way of appearing to do something rather than actually doing it.** (paragraph 5)

In what type of context would the above expressions be more appropriate than the ones used in the report?

The king of...

In this report the salmon is referred to as 'the king of freshwater fish'. In other contexts, the lion is often referred to as 'the king of the jungle', and the eagle as 'the king of birds'. What qualities do you think are being suggested by the use of this phrase?

What creatures might be referred to as:

- the king of the seas
- the king of the desert
- the king of the forest?

C Discussion

Is there an official body or organization in your country that is in charge of rivers or lakes? Are there any environmental groups that concern themselves with this issue? Why is it important to have clean river or lake

Poison lays waste to salmon river

By Robert Bedlow

HUNDREDS of thousands of fish have been killed on a 14-mile stretch of the River Eden in Cumbria, one of England's finest trout and salmon rivers, after liquid fertiliser leaked into the water.

The Eden was in danger of becoming "dead" and it would take at least three years for life to return, experts said yesterday.

Salmon, trout and most of the coarse fish died, including eels which are more resistant to pollution.

The accident happened on Saturday when a muck spreader overturned as a tanker, carrying ammonium hydroxide, was transferring its load at Lower Musgrave, near Kirkby Stephen.

The highly toxic substance seeped through the ground into Ploughland beck, which feeds into the Eden.

Mr Leslie Hughes, the National Rivers Authority pollution control manager in Cumbria, said: "It is the worst incident to my knowledge in Cumbria."

Last night the authority, which admitted it blundered after the accident, was attempting to neutralise the poison which was still killing fish as it neared Penrith.

A spokesman said: "We dammed the river to the north and south of the spillage and the fire brigade drained out the water to prevent further leakage.

"But in the evening, after samples had been taken, it was thought safe to remove the dams. Shortly afterwards, however, it was noticed that fish were dying, but it was too late to re-dam the beck.

"Staff have been monitoring the ammonia ever since. We are putting hydrochloric acid into the river to reduce the levels of the ammonia. This combined with a dilution effect from the waters of one of its tributaries, the river Eamont, will neutralise the ammonia and hopefully make the Eden safer."

Mr James Carr, regional representative of the Salmon & Trout Association, said it appeared that only a small quantity of the chemical had been spilled but it had killed all fish, including adult salmon and salmon parr.

The NRA said it was investigating the accident. "If there is a prosecution and someone is found to be negligent, we can ask for compensation to be paid to re-stock the river," said a spokesman.

The Daily Telegraph – 30 March 1993

water? What effects on health can polluted river water have? How would you set about starting an environmental pressure group on this issue?

Poison lays waste to salmon river

A The cause of death

1 Explain why the River Eden is in danger of becoming 'dead'.

2 Describe the steps taken to neutralize the poison.

B Language focus

Choosing to be personal...

Rewrite the following sentences using a personal pronoun:

(a) It was thought safe to remove the dams.
(b) It was noticed that fish were dying.

...or impersonal

Use the pronoun 'it' to make the following sentences impersonal:

(c) We felt they had made a mistake.
(d) She felt they had blundered.
(e) They said the workers had been careless.

Why do you think, in paragraph 9 of the article, the spokesman for the NRA uses sentences (a) and (b) above?

What sort of considerations would lead to the choice of the personal rather than the impersonal construction?

Hitting the headlines

Below are some alternative headlines for the article. Compare them with the original and suggest reasons why the writer chose that particular one.

(a) Poison kills fish in river
(b) The National Rivers Authority blunders
(c) Cumbria's worst pollution incident
(d) Ammonia gets into river

Why did they say that?

Look at the list of expressions used in the article, and say why they were chosen by the various speakers in preference to the possible alternatives:

article	**possible alternative**
incident (paragraph 6)	thing that's happened
monitoring (paragraph 10)	checking
combined with (paragraph 10)	together with
investigating (paragraph 12)	looking into

Looking for synonyms

Replace the word or words in bold in the following sentences with the word or words used in the article:

(a) The damage was caused by an **extremely poisonous** substance. (paragraph 5)
(b) The poison **soaked** through the ground. (paragraph 5)
(c) The Authority admitted it had **made a gross mistake**. (paragraph 7)
(d) Staff have been **checking** the poison levels. (paragraph 10)
(e) They attempted to **counteract** the effect of the ammonia. (paragraph 7)

Why do you think (d) and (e) were not used in the statement reported in the article?

C Role play

Split up into three groups, one to represent the National Rivers Authority, one the Salmon and Trout Association, and one the parents of children who bathe or swim in the river. Each group is to prepare an argument to present in a debate organized by the local television station about the accident. Choose a spokesperson from each group and someone to be the television presenter, and ask the rest of the class to put questions to them, with the television presenter acting as chairperson.

British Studies: how to protect the water environment

The picture below is taken from one of the many hand-outs and fact sheets published by the National Rivers Authority – Thames Region on how to appreciate and protect the water environment.

Examples of possible pollution sources

1 Illegal dumping of harmful chemicals.
2 Leakage of chemicals from industrial premises.
3 Illegal oil discharges from launches and ships.
4 Trade effluent discharges containing toxic waste.
5 Oil spillages from road tankers
6 Poor quality sewage works effluent.
7 Chemical spillages on the highway.
8 Liquid farmyard waste.
9 Liquor from farmyard silage stores.
10 Heating oil spillages and leaks from storage tanks.
11 Illegal disposal of car engine oil into drains.
12 Shopping trolleys and household debris.

The National Rivers Authority

Over to you

In the classroom

1 Look at the picture giving examples of possible sources of pollution, and identify the type reported in the newspaper article in the previous section.

2 Of the sources listed, say which ones are accidental and which ones deliberate.

3 Which type do you think is the most easily preventable?

4 Name as many sports or leisure pursuits as you can think of that can be practised or enjoyed on or by a river.

An outside project

Group target: to present as full a picture as possible of the purposes for which rivers are used in your country, and what measures are taken to protect them from pollution.

Work either individually or in pairs, depending on the number of people in the group, to carry out the following tasks:

1 Try to establish which organization or individual has responsibility for looking after rivers, and collect detailed information on rivers as:

(a) sources of water
(b) leisure facilities
(c) wildlife habitats

2 Make a list of the actual sources of river pollution in your country and put them in order of seriousness.

3 Find out what measures are taken to control the aspects of pollution you have noted.

Cardiac patients and relatives

Background

Harefield Hospital is a world famous National Health Service Trust hospital in Middlesex, near London. It specializes in heart and lung disorders.

Pre-viewing

Given that heart operations usually require a lengthy stay in hospital, can you suggest what problems this might cause for the following groups of people, especially if the hospital is a long way from the patient's home:

(a) child patients
(b) the patient's relatives

Video

A One problem after another

1 Describe the particular problems faced by the Carr family.

2 Describe the problems that cardiac operations on young children pose for their families.

3 What problems do heart operations pose for the hospital?

B Language focus

Doing your bit

You are keen to help the hospital, and would like to prepare a single-sheet handout asking people to support the appeal. Look at the lists below, and select the features you think would be appropriate for this.

grammar	vocabulary	punctuation
passives	medical jargon	commas
conditionals	long words	dashes
imperatives	short words	exclamation marks
relative clauses	adverbs	inverted commas
simple sentences	adjectives	question marks

Suggest an eye-catching headline.

How can you tell?

Look at paragraph 7 of the transcript. Several features of the grammar, and certain expressions would not have been used if this text had originally been written rather than spoken. Try to identify at least three.

What's the alternative?

What alternative word is used in the text for the following:

(a) the money that is needed to provide a service (paragraph 5)
(b) other children in the family (paragraph 7)

Why did the hospital spokeswoman prefer the word she used to (b) above?

What's your opinion?

In the left-hand column below are expressions that were used in the video, and next to them, possible alternatives. Suggest why the person who used the expression chose that particular one.

- loved ones (paragraph 1) family
- mother (paragraph 3) parent
- accommodation (paragraph 4) lodgings

C Discussion

Would you want to be near a relative of yours who had had a heart operation? Describe the sort of difficulties that would be caused by having to move into hospital for three months. How would you spend each day? What are the problems if a family has to be split up? What would happen if there were other children at school?

Live-wire heart operation saves a baby's life

By Peter Pallot, Health Services Staff

THE LIFE of a three-month old baby has been saved by surgeons in the first operation of its kind in the world, during which they used a burst of electricity along a half-inch wire to burn a hole in a blocked heart valve.

Details were given yesterday of the six-hour operation carried out at Groby Road Hospital, Leicester.

"Previous attempts have used too big a charge, generating too much heat, causing the operation to fail," said Dr Chen Chan, paediatric cardiologist, who carried out the operation.

A catheter was inserted in the groin and guided by X-ray to the blocked atrial valve, between Jessica Cooledge's heart and lungs. A five-watt burst of electricity was switched through the wire for three seconds.

A cold saline solution was injected into the artery from the other side of the blockage to cool the delicate tissue.

Dr Chan said the hot wire technique used readily-available equipment and was much cheaper than laser surgery, which cost about £2,500 for the hire of a machine for a day.

The final stage in the surgery was to widen the artery to restore the blood flow using a small balloon which was inflated at the site of the blockage.

The procedure meant Jessica did not need to have potentially-dangerous open-heart surgery.

Jessica's mother, Ms Sarah Cooledge, 17, of North Evington, Leicester, said: "Jessica is a very lucky baby — the live wire baby. I cannot thank the doctors enough. They were just brilliant."

She said she and her boyfriend, Mr Eric Marshall, 20, were devastated when told Jessica had been born with the rare malformation, pulmonary atresia.

Jessica was sent home within days of the operation last month.

"We are keeping an eye on her to make sure she stays pink," said Dr Chan.

"There was some risk but, if it was my own child, I would have gone ahead. So far as I know, we are the first to successfully use this technique in the entire world.

"I've seen Jessica recently and she is great."

Dr Doug Skehan, consultant cardiologist, and Dr Shakeel Qureshi, of Guy's Hospital in London, also took part in the operation.

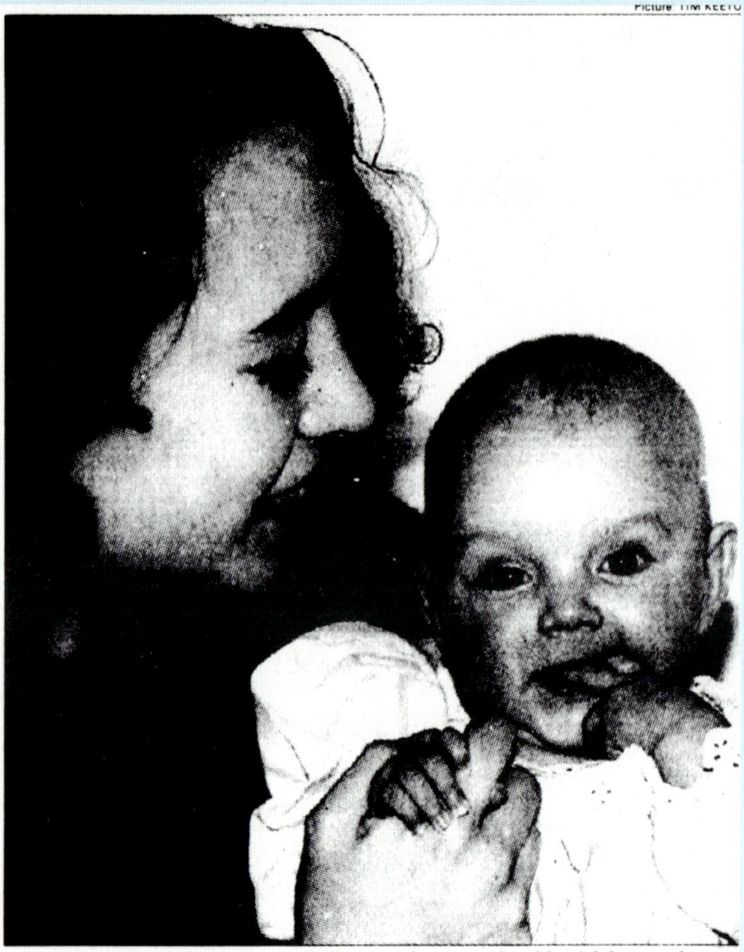

'Very lucky girl': Jessica Cooledge, now four months old, with her mother

The Daily Telegraph – 17 January 1992

Live-wire heart operation saves a baby's life

A Getting down to essentials

Below are ten sentences giving details of the operation. Reduce them to four.

1 The operation lasted six hours.

2 A catheter was inserted into the groin.

3 It was guided by x-ray to the blocked valve.

4 A burst of electricity was switched through the wire.

5 This lasted for three seconds.

6 The wire was half an inch long.

7 A cold saline solution was injected into the artery.

8 The purpose of this was to cool the tissue.

9 The artery was widened to restore the blood flow.

10 A small balloon was used.

B Language focus

A letter to the parents...

You are a consultant about to perform the live-wire operation on a child, and intend to write to the parents explaining what you are going to do. Look at paragraphs 4 and 5 where the relevant information is given, and pick out the dominant linguistic feature. What difference do you think the letter form will make to the way you give the information? (seventy to eighty words)

A question of style

Compare paragraphs 1, 2, 4, 5 and 11 with paragraphs 9, 10, 12, 13, and 14. How is the formality of the style related to the subject matter? What grammatical features emphasize these different styles?

Doctor and patient

In each of the pairs of sentences below, the first one is more common than the second as a standard hospital response to an enquiry about a patient. What impression does thc surgeon give by being less formal?

(a) We are keeping her under observation.
We are keeping an eye on her.

(b) I've seen Jessica recently and she is making good progress.
I've seen Jessica recently and she is great.

Cutting down on words

The following are paraphrases in the infinitive of verbs which occur in the text. What are the verbs?

(a) to be unsuccessful (paragraph 3)
(b) to make wider (paragraph 7)
(c) to fill with air (paragraph 7)

Give a reason why (b) and (c) were not used in the text.

C Discussion

Would you let a child of yours have an operation that had never been performed before? How would you feel if the operation had been done before, but had failed?

Lasers in dentistry

Background

There are three types of dental patient in Britain: National Health Service (NHS) patients, private patients, and insurance scheme patients. The NHS provides a free service for children, nursing mothers, and people on low incomes, and reduced costs for other people. Private patients pay the full cost of all treatment. Insurance scheme patients are entitled to certain types of treatment from their dentist in exchange for a regular monthly premium paid to the insurance company.

Pre-viewing

General reaction

What is the usual reaction to the idea of a visit to the dentist? What sorts of emotions does this topic raise? Pinpoint the precise areas of dislike.

Specific reaction

Does the idea that a laser can be used in dentistry make you feel more, or less confident about a visit to the dentist?

Video

A In the dentist's chair

1 What percentage of people visit their dentist regularly?

2 Why are people afraid of visiting the dentist?

3 What can the laser be used for?

4 Where was the laser made?

5 How much does it cost?

B Language focus

What is a chairside manner?

The television reporter uses 'chairside manner' to sum up a dentist's way of relating to patients, by analogy with 'bedside manner', which refers to the way doctors relate to their patients.

From the information given in the clip, make notes explaining the uses of the new laser which can later be filled out for use by a dentist with an 'accomplished chairside manner'. (paragraph 2)

Can you explain it?

Look at the two sets of expressions below. What aspects of a visit to the dentist was the reporter trying to emphasize in choosing the left-hand ones rather than those on the right?

- a traumatic experience (paragraph 1) a very unpleasant experience
- the steeliest nerve (paragraph 2) the bravest person

Speech and writing

'People, when they come to me, are always very, very nervous,' is what the dentist says. How would you re-arrange his words if they had been intended for a written context?

Something unexpected

Find the phrase in the transcript that corresponds to the following definition, and say why you think the reporter chose to use it in preference to the definition:

- advantages other than those planned or expected

C Role play

With a partner, act the parts of a very nervous patient and a dentist. As the patient, find out what your dentist intends to do, ask about the cost, and ask if it will hurt. As the dentist, try to reassure the patient, and show him or her the new laser and explain how it works.

In a church crypt in central London, a dentist is providing care and advice for down-and-outs. Alan Jabez talks to her about the work

Filling a gap for the homeless and toothless

MONDAY afternoon, and the queue outside Blanaid Daly's dental clinic is growing ever longer. Many of the patients have been watching the lunchtime television programmes while others have come off the street to grab a hot cup of tea.

The waiting area is a room deep below the ground containing a couple of old chairs, while the clinic doubles as an office and doctor's surgery at other times. The only medical equipment is an old chiropodist's chair; a wobbly table lamp provides the illumination.

Once a week Ms Daly establishes a temporary dental clinic here in the crypt beneath St Martin-in-the-Fields church in Trafalgar Square. She provides basic treatment to many homeless people who have not visited a dental surgery in years, and whose teeth are often in appalling conditions.

The first patient is Bob, a fit-looking man in his fifties who used to be a boxer. Most of his front teeth are either missing or have been badly smashed, and he has come to pick up a new set of dentures.

Ms Daly, who does not wear a white coat so as not to create barriers between her and the patients, talks to him about his general condition, as well as asking whether he has found a job and a place to stay. As he has been to the surgery before, he feels he can trust Ms Daly, and appreciates her concern and advice.

Unfortunately, the new dentures do not quite fit, so Ms Daly says she will take them home, make a few alterations, and then make a special journey back to St Martin's the following day.

Such commitment has earned her the respect of her patients. Many complain that the rest of society largely ignores them or treats them with extreme caution. Ms Daly feels that providing support and giving extra time to patients should be the priority of every health worker irrespective of whether they are being paid.

She moved to London from Dublin a couple of years ago, eager to pursue her interest in community health. She receives a grant from the homelessness charity Crisis, which is best known for organising a massive "open Christmas" for homeless people in a disused warehouse in central London each year, but is increasingly providing support services for the homeless throughout the year.

Each week Ms Daly visits a number of local community centres where homeless people go, offering whatever dental care she can. Most places are even more basic than the St Martin's clinic, she says: "I'll usually have to clear away coffee cups and cigarette ends before I can begin."

She feels that many of her growing number of patients prefer the basic facilities. "As they are in a territory they are familiar with, it often helps to de-stigmatise their perception of a typical surgery," she says.

Before establishing the mobile clinic – she carries all her supplies and instruments on the underground – she visited many community centres in London to gain a better understanding of the problems and conditions of homeless people, of whom there are now many thousand throughout the capital. "I felt it was very important to get to know them first and also to gain their trust," she says.

The idea seems to have worked. These days, a little over a year since she began, she is finding that people are coming back for return visits, and many are keen to open up and talk about all their problems.

She is well aware that for some lonely homeless people, the chance of having an ordinary conversation can be as valuable as the relief of a minor toothache. She also finds herself offering advice about housing or how to fill in forms and pay important bills.

As she does not have a dental nurse, Ms Daly has to perform a range of duties. When she sees new patients, she dictates their dental condition into a cassette recorder and transcribes the tape at home. She also has to sterilise her instruments at home.

Some people survive with no dentures at all, seeing an unhealthy mouth as a hazard of life on the street

At all the community centres she displays notices telling people the days and times she will be in attendance. She then operates a queuing system, as well as making appointments – aiming to use the time as well as possible.

The vast majority of her patients are men, their ages ranging from the early twenties to the late seventies. Many have teeth in such bad condition – usually caused by dietery problems or a complete lack of care – that they have become afraid of visiting a normal surgery.

Most have teeth broken or missing and many also have excessive plaque, tartar and broken fillings. Another typical problem is dentures that are either badly fitted or broken, resulting in the person having difficulty speaking or eating. Some people she has seen have managed to survive with no dentures at all, accepting an unhealthy mouth as one of the hazards of life on the street.

No matter how bad any person's teeth, she never insists on specific action. "I make recommendations and then let the individuals decide what action they want to take themselves," she says.

Her reasoning is that as most homeless people have so many other physical and emotional problems to deal with, spending time getting their teeth sorted out often comes low down on their list of priorities.

The St Martin's clinic is the one where Ms Daly has become best known. There is usually a rush of patients to see her. In the waiting room, a scuffle breaks out between men vying to be next in line. Some are slightly drunk, while others are unshaven and poorly dressed.

One man pushes his way to the front but is removed by one of the permanent staff – always on the look-out to make sure Ms Daly is all right. There is a panic button in the surgery, but she has never had to use it. She feels confident that her relaxed style and Irish banter will get her out of any tight situation.

When she is unable to carry out treatment, she makes an appointment with a local dentist who has a fully equipped clinic and is sympathetic to her efforts.

Initially, the general response from other dentists was that they did not want hordes of unkempt men hanging around their waiting rooms. But gradually she has found a more favourable attitude, and an increasing number of dentists are now keen to offer their services – especially if the patients have been sent by Ms Daly.

Rather than "dropping" their NHS patients, as many dentists are currently threatening to do, Ms Daly would like them to increase their NHS workloads and welcome homeless people to their practices.

She opposes the idea of establishing special services for the homeless, unless they have acute mental or medical problems, believing that such action would alienate then further from the rest of society.

She would like to see the Crisis project expanded across Britain. Her ultimate aim is to ensure that homeless people everywhere can receive the same dental care that the rest of us take for granted.

Sadly, in today's profit-hungry health world her goal seems increasingly idealistic.

The Independent – 3 September 1992

Filing a gap for the homeless and toothless

A The general picture

Where does Ms Daly hold her Monday afternoon clinic, and who are her patients?

More details

1 Describe the various ways in which Ms Daly helps her patients. (paragraphs 9, 13, 18, 22)

2 State her ultimate aim. (paragraph 26)

B Language focus

Making comparisons

Work in pairs with one of each pair writing an impartial account of the differences between Ms Daly's practice and the one shown in the video, and the other an emotional account of the differences, focusing on the misfortunes of the underprivileged. (eighty words)

Afterwards, compare your accounts and make notes of how they differ in the types of construction and vocabulary used.

What's in a title?

Below is a list of alternative titles for the article. Compare them with the original and suggest why the original is the most appropriate:

(a) Dentistry for the homeless
(b) Dentist works with down-and-outs
(c) Mobile dental clinics for the homeless

What were they really worried about?

(a) 'hordes of unkempt men hanging around their waiting rooms'
(b) 'lots of untidy looking men in their waiting rooms'

Why was (a) rather than (b) the initial response from other dentists? What fears of other dentists about helping the homeless are suggested by the use of 'hordes' and 'hanging around'?

On home ground

Why do you think Ms Daly uses the word 'territory' rather than 'place' in paragraph 10 when contrasting the crypt with a proper dental surgery?

C Discussion

Do you agree with Ms Daly's reasons for not wearing a white coat? Do you think that homeless people are right when they say that the rest of society ignores them? If so, why do you think this happens, and what can be done about it?

Role play

You are a spokesperson for a charity concerned with the problem of homelessness. You are being interviewed on television and have one minute in which to convince viewers that both society and the individual are responsible for helping those in need. What will you say?

British Studies: attitudes to dental care

The Oxfordshire Family Health Services Authority conducted a dental survey in the summer of 1992 to examine the local adult population's attitudes and beliefs about dental care. They wanted to highlight the things that might prevent people from seeking dental care, and their survey revealed that for many people, anxiety and cost were the main obstacles. Below are some statistics about anxiety.

Table A summarizes the respondents' level of agreement to a set of statements made by people about visiting the dentist, and Table B gives a percentage breakdown by social class of those who definitely agreed about always feeling anxious.

Note: the social classes, for the purposes of this survey, were divided into classes I, II, III non-manual, III manual, IV and V. The usual groupings are 1 and 2 professional/managerial, 3 white collar non-manual, 4 skilled manual, 5 unskilled manual/pensioners.

Table A: anxiety	**Definitely agree %**	**Agree to some extent %**	**Do not agree %**	**Don't know %**
I'd like to know more about what the dentist is going to do and why.	35	37	25	3
I'm nervous of some kinds of dental treatment.	31	39	27	2
The pain of it. I don't like being hurt.	27	43	28	2
I always feel anxious about going to the dentist.	29	36	34	2
The worst part of going to the dentist is the waiting.	20	33	45	2
It's embarrassing to admit that I haven't been to the dentist for so long.	17	16	62	5
If I had toothache I'd rather take pain-killers than go to the dentist.	7	10	82	2

The Oxfordshire Family Health Services Authority

Table B: definately agree 'always feel anxious' by social class

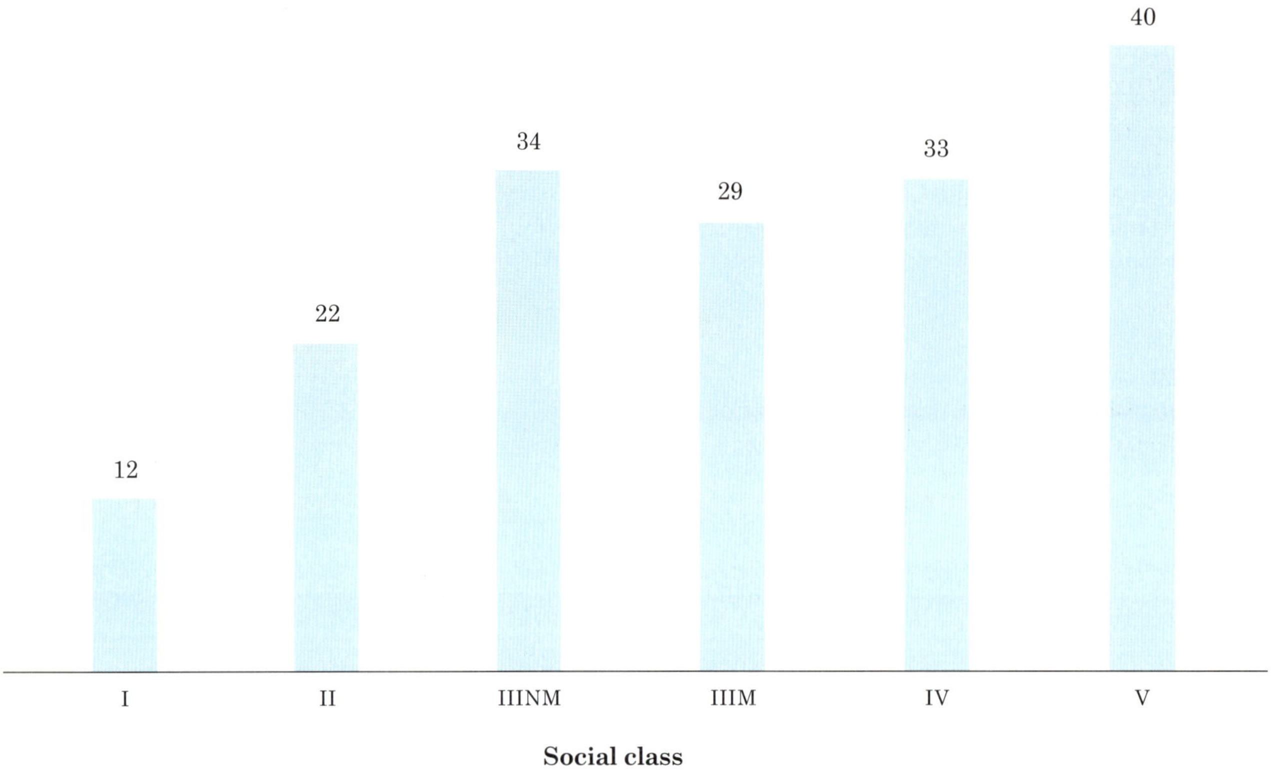

The Oxfordshire Family Health Services Authority

Over to you

In the classroom

1 Each member of the class/group is to respond to the set of statements in Table A, then the whole group is to work out a set of percentages for 'definitely agree', and 'agree to some extent' for both males and females.

2 Consult together in pairs to suggest two other things that might cause anxiety about a visit to the dentist, then compare your findings together as a group.

3 Can you think of a reason why the proportion of people who always feel anxious about a visit to the dentist should be highest in class 5, and lowest in class 1?

4 Suggest ways in which anxiety could be minimized by the people or in the places listed below:

(a) the dentist
(b) the dental receptionist
(c) the waiting room
(d) the surgery

An outside project

The Oxford project was a survey of adult attitudes to dental care. As a group, conduct a similar survey among teenagers aged sixteen to eighteen. First, agree on a set of questions that will elicit the following information:

(a) if they visit the dentist and how often
(b) if they go just for treatment or also for regular check-ups
(c) if they feel any anxiety about going, and if so, the specific cause of the anxiety

Then prepare a questionnaire that will have spaces on it for the respondents to fill in their age and sex. Try to get at least thirty teenagers (fifteen male; fifteen female) to complete the questionnaire, and then produce a set of statistics to reply to the following:

1 Whether more males or females of the age of sixteen visit the dentist.

2 What proportion of teenagers are affected by the 'anxiety' element, and whether this varies with age and sex.

3 Whether more females than males go for regular check-ups, and if this varies with age and sex.

Indian pupils come top

Background

Certain areas of England such as London, the Midlands, and Bradford in the North have large ethnic populations. By contrast, the number of teachers from ethnic backgrounds is very small. Certain ethnic groups seem to do better than others in the field of educational achievement.

Pre-viewing

Does doing well in school depend entirely on being clever? What can parents do to help? What part is played by teachers? What roles, if any, do social background and religion play in examination success?

Video

A Top of the class

Fill in the blanks in the following sentences:

1 The results of .... pupils were studied.

2 The survey was based on the examination results of sixteen year-olds ....

3 The best results were scored by Indian pupils from ....

4 The survey found that ...... and .... are the main factors in determining examination results.

5 Children from more .... communities did less well.

6 Schools need to work with parents to raise their ...... of what their children are ...... of ....

B Language focus

The end of term report

You are a head teacher from a school in a poor area with a mix of children from different ethnic backgrounds. You want to write a general report for all the parents explaining the poor results and suggesting ways they can help. The expressions listed below contain the ideas you would like to put across, but are too difficult. What will you write that will be easier for non-native speakers of English to understand?

- achievement levels, middle-class backgrounds, self-esteem, parental expectations, socially deprived, parental involvement, dominant factors, continued improvement

What was the response?

Paragraphs 3 and 4 of the transcript give different responses to the survey. In the light of the information given in paragraph 2 about the contents of the survey, which do you think is the more relevant response? Give reasons for your answer.

Why did he say that?

Suggest reasons why the reporter used the expressions on the left, rather than their equivalents on the right:

- the two most dominant factors — the two main reasons
- more socially deprived — poorer
- increased achievement levels — better results

It's not as simple as that

For each of the words listed below, the transcript (paragraph 2) uses longer or more formal words. See if you can identify them, and explain why they were used.

- deciding, mainly, got, did

C Discussion

What part does parental expectation play in the education of children? Are good teachers more important than involved parents?

Nicholas Pyke reports on figures the DFE has refused to release

Survey finds ethnic staff in a minority

Ethnic-minority groups are seriously under-represented among the country's teachers, according to confidential Government figures obtained by The TES.

Figures gathered over two years as part of a Government monitoring programme suggest that only 3.3 per cent of full-time teachers come from minority groups.

This compares with an estimated 5.5 per cent of the population who come from ethnic minorities. The Runnymede Trust, however, believes that minority groups make up 8 per cent of pupils in schools and that the proportion is rising.

This week the Commission for Racial Equality accused the Government of lacking political will to conclude its survey and publish the findings. So far, the programme has only obtained ethnic figures for two thirds of teachers. Ministers have refused to release the figures.

The survey was recommended in the 1985 Swann Report into under-achievement among black and Asian pupils. But the Department for Education still has no reliable picture either of teacher or pupil population, according to the CRE. The Swann Report said the lack of black and Asian teachers was a significant factor in poor academic results.

Under-representation is particularly acute in some areas. In Bradford, for example, around one third of pupils are black or Asian and education officials think this may rise to half by the year 2000. This is matched by less than 1 per cent of teachers.

Eric Forth, the schools minister, has told Parliament that the figures are not publicly available because the local authorities have not all yet replied.

Phil Barnett, a CRE principal officer, said: "We're disappointed at the lack of apparent priority accorded to all ethnic monitoring resulting from DFE circulars, both of teacher employment and children."

"Ethnic monitoring is a cornerstone of any equal opportunities' policy. We would want to see it enshrined in every aspect of the DFE's guidance and work. This should be established in the current Education Bill and we will be seeking an amendment in the House of Lords to that effect."

The lack of minority recruits to teacher training is a long-standing problem. Figures are, again, hard to come by, but those supplied by the Graduate Teacher Training Registry suggest that only 4.8 per cent of applications to post-graduate courses came from minority groups in 1991 and 4.7 per cent of acceptances. This is well below both applications and acceptances for higher education overall, suggesting that teacher training is particularly unpopular.

The Government's own recruitment quango, TASC – Teaching As a Career – admits as much. Its director, Jack Dodds, speculates that the experience of racism in the classroom may deter potential applicants.

The Higher Education Funding Council this week confirmed that it will be giving £500,000 to initiatives encouraging black and Asian graduates to enter teacher training.

A number of universities and teacher-training colleges already run courses specifically to attract black and Asian applicants. At the University of North London, for example, 40 per cent of education students are from ethnic minorities – thought by the staff to be the biggest proportion in the country.

This is the result of 10 years' hard work, says Dr Greg Condry, dean of the education department. He urges caution against quick-fix solutions. Much of the university's success is based on its reputation among minor-ity groups, who enter the course con-fident of a fair deal.

Bradford education authority is itself sponsoring an articled teacher scheme from next September, specifically to attract black and Asian applicants.

Another difficulty is the low esteem in which teaching is held by Asian families. It is seen as "a second-class profession", says Moeen Yaseen, education adviser to the Islamia Schools Trust. Even Muslim schools, he says, do not have enough Muslim teachers.

Times Educational Supplement –
12 March 1993

Survey finds ethnic staff in a minority

A What are their views?

Complete the following sentences as briefly as possible in your own words:

1 The Runnymede Trust believes ....

2 The Swann Report said ....

3 Education officials in Bradford think ....

4 Figures supplied by the Graduate Teacher Training Registry suggest ....

5 The Higher Education Council confirmed ....

B Language focus

Attracting applicants

You have been asked to draft an information sheet designed to attract ethnic minority recruits into teaching, and you want to stress the following: good career opportunities; doing a worthwhile job; and creating a more balanced educational system. Which of the following might you want to avoid, and why?

- negative statements
- passives
- comparisons
- simple sentences
- reported speech
- colons
- exclamation marks
- inverted commas
- question marks
- capital letters

- questions forms
- personal pronouns
- racist vocabulary
- educational jargon
- adjectives

Making comparisons

The Swann Report suggests that lack of ethnic staff plays a significant part in underachievement among black and Asian pupils. How does this compare with the findings of ILEA's survey which was the subject of the video report?

How would you explain it?

Rewrite the following sentences in a way which explains the meaning of the words in bold:

(a) The Department for Education still has no **reliable picture.**

(b) Under representation is **particularly acute** in some areas.

(c) The lack of **minority recruits** is a long-standing problem.

(d) The experience of racism may **deter potential applicants.**

What did it say in the article?

Choose the words or phrases from the article that match the following definitions:

(a) discrimination against people because of ethnic origin (paragraph 11)

(b) an organization funded by the government for a specific job (paragraph 11)

(c) plans of action designed to solve problems speedily (paragraph 14)

(d) something that is of prime importance (paragraph 8)

What contrast does the speaker stress by using his phrase instead of (c)? Is anything else implied by his expression?

C Discussion

How are ethnic minorities treated in your country from the educational point of view? Is use of the mother tongue allowed in school? Is any attempt made to attract students from ethnic minorities into teaching? What provision, if any, is made in school for the children of non-dominant cultures to practise their religion?

Teacher stress

Background

There have been several major changes to the English educational system over the last few years, relating not only to what is taught, but also to the management and funding of schools. The changes most directly affecting teachers have been the introduction of the National Curriculum with its ten core subjects, and the compulsory testing of pupils at various stages of their school life.

Pre-viewing

1 Name two groups of people that can cause stress to teachers.

2 Suggest ways in which stress can affect health.

3 Can you think of ways in which the teaching unions could help?

Video

A Fill in the blanks in the following summary of the report:

The Health and Safety Commission's report says that ...... pupils and aggressive ...... are causing serious ...... among teachers. The ...... education changes have added to the pressures, and many teachers are unable to .... The NUT offers ...... but often things have gone too far. The report ...... that ...... of teachers become seriously ill, with another ...... having less serious .... There is a feeling that stress is to do with ......, and also that the situation would be better if ...... were more ...... with the changes taking place.

B Language focus

A challenging profession?

You are a teacher who had to leave the profession because of stress, and are annoyed by the Department of Education's remarks given in the last paragraph of the transcript. Using the information given in paragraphs 2 and 5, write a very personal account of the stresses and challenges of life in the classroom (sixty to seventy words). Afterwards, check the list below and say which of the linguistic features you used and why.

- questions, general statements, personal pronouns, passives, imperatives, possessive pronouns, modifiers, relative clauses, perfect tense, reported speech, negatives

Another way of saying it

Paragraph 3 is a transcript of a perfectly acceptable spoken text. How would you rearrange it to suggest that the speaker's words were less spontaneous and more carefully chosen?

What's your opinion?

Why do you think the speaker in paragraph 8 repeated 'we think' three times, instead of using 'also' or 'in addition' to begin his second and third sentences?

An unusual context?

In paragraph 2, teachers are referred to as 'casualties'. Can you suggest two more usual contexts for the word rather than the classroom? What aspect of the situation is the report trying to stress by using this word?

C Discussion

In the video report it is claimed that stress is a management issue. Suggest ways in which the government and head teachers could help to reduce the burdens falling on teachers. Can you think of ways in which teachers could be protected from aggressive parents?

Jobs are chief cause of stress

By David Fletcher, Health Services Correspondent

Job worries, followed by money troubles and anxiety about children, were the greatest single causes of stress, a survey by BUPA, the private health care group, said yesterday.

The survey of 700 people throughout Britain discovered that concern about health caused nearly one in four people to become stressful, while one in eight said their relatives were a source of stress.

Men put worries about their job at the top of the list of stress factors.

Women, on the other hand, were certain that it was their children who caused them the most concern. The irritating factors of modern life – noisy neighbours, fear of crime and other people's cigarette smoke – all came near the bottom of the list of stress-causing factors.

But one in 20 people said Christmas and New Year were a major source of stress and a similar proportion blamed noise generated by traffic, aeroplanes and roadworks.

People said that they reacted to stress by becoming more irritable, impatient or angry.

Other effects included having difficulty in sleeping, becoming tired, getting headaches and being generally unhappy. Some reacted by increasing their smoking, eating more or taking medication.

The most popular solution to stress was talking to someone about it or trying to deal with the cause.

Others said they went to bed, took a holiday or simply took a break from work.

Dr Hugh Thelwall-Jones, BUPA group medical director, said the survey showed that the things which caused most stress were personal matters such as a job, income and family.

"While it is significant that more external factors such as noise, crime and commuting are adding to the aggravation of our lives, they are perhaps considered less contributory to stress because they are beyond our control and in a sense we have a higher tolerance of them." But he said it was worrying that so many people ate or smoked more when they were under stress. "On top of being tired and irritable, these responses cannot help their general state of health and may become habits that are continued beyond the period of stress," said Dr Thelwall-Jones.

The Daily Telegraph – 18 April 1992

What causes the stress you suffer?

	All	Male	Female	Scotland: North	Midlands: SW Wales	London: SE Anglia
	%	%	%	%	%	%
Job	33	48	23	23	33	37
Financial problems	29	30	29	29	28	32
Health	23	21	23	23	18	24
Relatives	13	6	17	17	11	12
Fear of unemployment	10	10	11	11	7	15
Relationship with partner	10	9	11	11	9	10
Others smoking	8	8	8	8	7	9
Elderly relatives	8	5	9	9	4	11
Fear of crime	7	6	7	7	7	6
Noisy neighbours	6	6	6	6	6	8
Commuting	6	11	3	3	8	6
Child's education	5	4	6	6	5	5
Christmas	5	5	5	5	3	5
Pollution	4	3	6	6	7	3
Noise	4	5	4	4	4	6
Nothing in particular	5	4	5	5	6	4
Other	12	1	13	13	10	14

What happens when you are under stress

Grow irritable	51%	Eat more	21%
Difficult sleeping	45%	Take medication	9%
Become tired	37%	Eat less	8%
Get headaches	36%	Prone to illness	8%
Generally unhappy	30%	Start drinking	6%
Become depressed	28%	Other	2%
Grow frustrated	25%	Nothing	2%
Smoke more	25%		

Jobs are chief cause of stress

A Causes...

1 Name the three main causes of stress.

2 How do things like pollution and noise contribute to stress?

...and effects

1 State the three main reactions to stress.

2 Why is it worrying that some people eat or smoke more when under stress?

B Language focus

Can you think why?

Work in pairs to write very brief accounts (fifty words) of why Christmas and New Year are seen as major causes of stress. One of you is absolutely certain why, but the other is not at all sure. List the words and phrases that are likely to be present in the account of the one who is uncertain, and absent from the other account.

What difference does it make?

- noise generated by traffic • noise caused by traffic
- beyond the period of stress • when the stress is over

Say in each case why you think the phrase on the left was used in preference to the alternative on the right.

Saying what was said, but differently

Below is a paraphrase of the medical director's comments in paragraph 11:

While it is worth noticing that outside things like noise, crime and commuting are adding to the problems of our lives, they are less likely to be thought of as causing stress because they are beyond our control and so we can put up with them better.

In which area of language has the changes been made? What is the overall effect of the changes? Suggest a context where the paraphrase would be more appropriate than the original.

The last word

Look at paragraph 11 of the article and write your own paraphrase of Dr Thelwall-Jones' comments. (forty-five to fifty words)

C Discussion

What are the problems associated with children at different stages of their life: as infants, as school children, as teenagers? If the survey had been conducted among teenagers instead of adults, what sort of things would have appeared under the heading of **causes?**

British Studies: problems for teachers in Britain

Below is a table charting the areas in which teachers experience problems. It was compiled from responses given by teachers themselves, based on the number of times a particular area was cited as a problem. The information was collected as part of a research project entitled *Teachers and schools: a study of organizational health and stress* undertaken on behalf of the National Union of Teachers. This was taken from one of their pamphlets entitled *Anti-racist curriculum guidelines.*

Table C: problem areas or domains

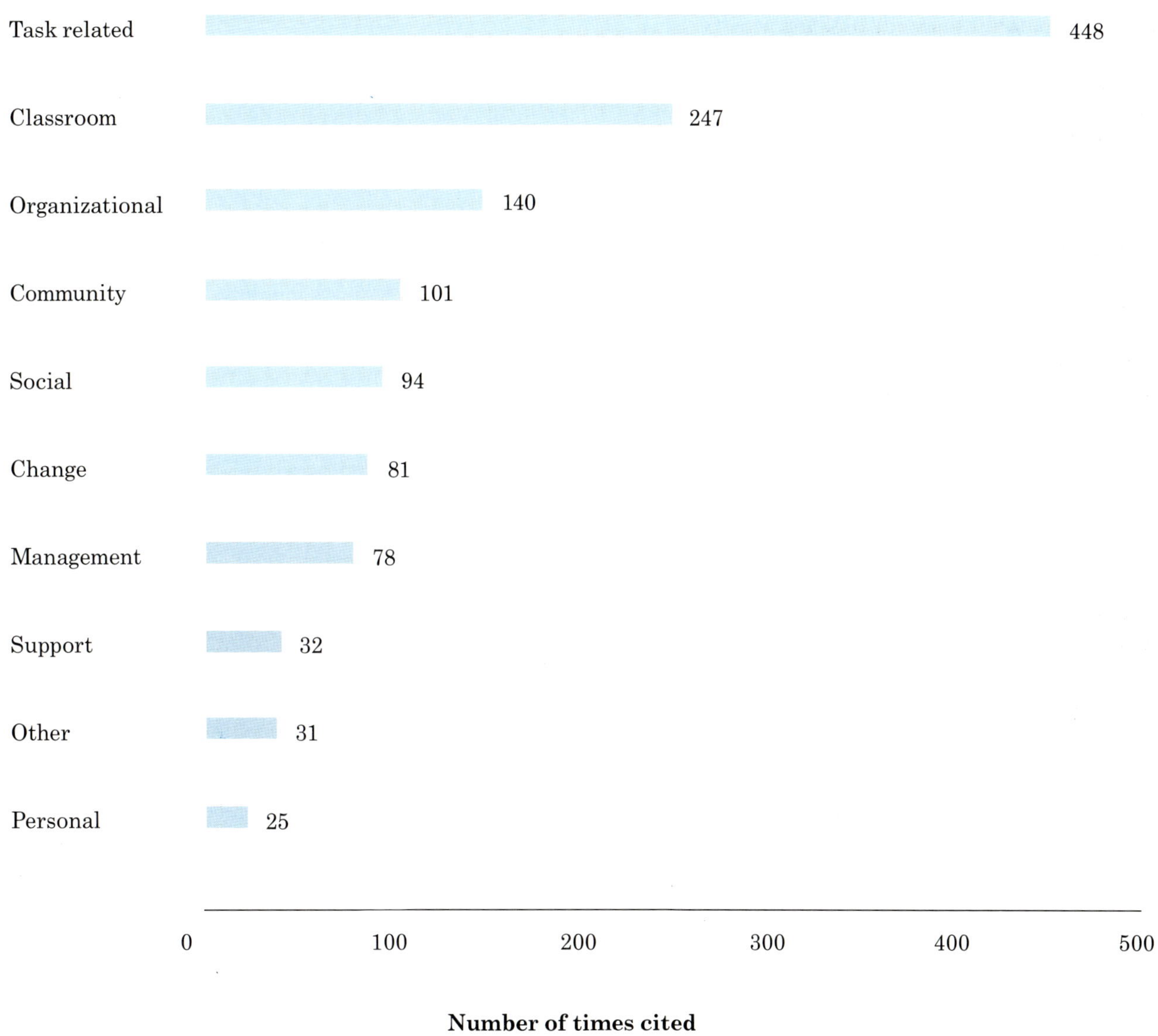

The National Union of Teachers

Over to you

In the classroom

1 Below is a list of possible causes of stress for teachers. Put each one in an appropriate category as given in the chart above, and where your categorization differs from that of others in the group, be prepared to justify your choice.

- Marking, disruptive pupils, extra-curricular duties, large classes, covering for absent teachers, aggressive parents, poor head teacher, lack of resources, new curriculum

2 Make a list of the extra-curricular activities undertaken by teachers at your school. Is there anything you would like to add to the list? Do you think teachers should be expected to do these activities?

3 Discuss how you think that a broadly-based curriculum could be made available to ethnic minority children, in the following subjects: music, foreign languages, English.

4 In what ways could respect for different cultural traditions be taught in schools? Do you think that religious education has a part to play in this area?

An outside project

Working as a group, try to discover as much as you can about the educational system in your own town or city by finding the answers to the following questions:

1 How are the schools managed – by central government, by local education authorities, by governing bodies, or by other means?

2 What qualifications are required for teaching, and how long does the training period last?

3 What is the social standing of the teacher in the community?

4 How does teachers' pay compare with that of other professions?

5 Are there any teaching unions?

6 What is the average class size in

(a) primary schools
(b) secondary schools?

7 How are problem children dealt with?

8 Does the problem of aggressive parents exist?

9 How do ethnic minorities fit into the system? Is any special provision made for them, with respect to religious practices, and language teaching?

Present the answers to these questions in the form of a written report.

Problems of the elderly

Background

As a result of better housing conditions and improved medical care, people are living longer. Men and women born between 1910–12 had an average life expectancy of fifty-three years. The average now is seventy-two years for men and seventy-eight years for women, and the care of the elderly is increasingly becoming an urgent social problem.

Pre-viewing

Look at the following quotation and then discuss the questions.

'Both as individuals and as members of society, we find it extremely difficult to be honest about our attitudes to old age and old people.' (*Aspects of ageism,* published by the Centre for Policy on Ageing)

As individuals do we fear old age, and avoid old people? Do we feel guilty or resentful about our response to the demands made on us by elderly relatives?

As a society, do we allocate enough resources to the care of the elderly, or do we regard it as a waste of money?

Video

A The general picture

Describe three features of Bertha's daily routine.

More details

1 What is Bertha celebrating?

2 When did she move into her house?

3 How many elderly people will there be by the year 2000?

4 What help does Bertha get from the State?

5 What help does Lily get?

B Language focus

The positive and the negative

Work in pairs to write down your impressions of old age, with one noting the positive aspects, and the other the negative ones. Afterwards, compare your versions to see how your opposing views are reflected in your choice of vocabulary and your use of personal and impersonal constructions.

The first impression

Do the first two sentences of the clip prepare you for the report that follows? Write two sentences that you think would more accurately prepare you for the report.

How would you have changed it?

Do you think television viewers would be moved to do something about the problems of elderly people by watching this news clip? What is the overall impression created by the report? If you had written the report and had wanted to stress the **problems** of old age, what changes would you make to the following:

(a) the type of elderly person interviewed
(b) the occasion of the hundredth birthday celebration
(c) some of the expressions used

The spoken word

Look at paragraph 3 of the transcript, and pick out three features that tell you that this was originally a spoken text.

C Discussion

What problems does an increasingly ageing population cause both for their relatives and the State? What services should the State provide for old people? How can the local community help?

Mobile Day Centre visits halls

In 1988 Age Concern Leomister began to research the number of elderly people living in north-west Herefordshire and the local services available to them. The research showed that almost 20 per cent of the population in this district were elderly and that there were common problems for them of transport, isolation and frailty, resulting in an appreciable reduction in their quality of life. To provide an answer to these needs, the idea of a Mobile Day Centre – offering a number of services – was developed.

A fortnightly rota has been established during which period the Mobile Day Centre, consisting of a minibus towing a caravan, visits eight village halls. About 130 members and 40 intermittent users are served. The minibus is used for transport to and from the hall and the caravan is used as a base for a number of services. Members meet in the hall and take part in a variety of craft and communal activities and, most importantly, have the opportunity to chat together. A hot meal is served at lunch-time.

Among the services provided are footcare, hairdressing, health checks, and advice on hearing problems. A variety of advisory services such as Citizens Advice Bureau and the Benefits Agency where privacy is required is also available. The WRVS arranges for lunches to be prepared locally and these are collected and delivered to the village hall by local volunteers.

Capital Funding was obtained from Help the Aged, the Rural Development Commission, Age Concern England and Telethon. Revenue funding for three years came from Joint Finance (Health and Social Services) and the Rural Development Commission. Each day centre also regularly engages in some form of fundraising activity especially to finance outings and to help with day to day costs. Additional benefits have included the involvement of the local community and the raising of the centres' profiles.

Staff

A number of Age Concern staff are involved. The project has a part-time organiser. There is also a driver who, because he attends each venue, is well-placed to deputise for the organiser, and a relief driver. Volunteer input is crucial to the scheme and, at each day centre, there is a volunteer leader and a deputy who, together with other volunteers, care for the elderly members. The volunteers benefit from monthly training sessions at Leominster and periodical sessions in their own villages.

Referrals to the day centre come from social services, home care staff, district nurses, health visitors and general practitioners. Useful information also comes informally from local shops and post offices, volunteers, relatives and friends. The referral criteria include isolation, disablement, mental confusion, frailty and support for carers.

A typical day begins with the Mobile Day Centre arriving at the village hall at 9 am. The minibus departs to collect the members and volunteers from the surrounding area. Coffee is served from 10 am and craft activities, games and exercises fill the rest of the morning. As well as providing nutrition, lunch together is an important social activity for elderly folk who usually eat alone. During the afternoon there is the opportunity to read books, look at newspapers and chat together before tea and the journey home at 3 pm. Throughout the day the caravan is used for the services previously mentioned. There are regular outings, maybe out to tea, or further afield for the day.

Unique

Age Concern Leominster consider their project to be unique in two significant respects. It has a built in 'flexibility factor' in that staff will initiate and support the establishment of a day centre, providing transport, services and facilities. However, the centre will be an integral part of the local community run by volunteers. Less support will be needed as time goes on, freeing Age Concern staff to develop new services in other areas. The second important aspect is that the day centre becomes part of the rural life of the area. Links are made with different local organisations and groups and the project belongs to the community rather than being imposed from outside.

This exciting project is of great benefit to elderly people in north-west Herefordshire. It helps to relieve problems of loneliness and isolation and offers companionship and practical advice. It helps communities provide support for their elderly inhabitants and respite for the carers. It should be an example and an inspiration to groups in other parts of the country.

Rural Viewpoint – April 1993
Issue no. 54

Note: WRVS stands for the Women's Royal Voluntary Service

Mobile Day Centre visits halls

A Problems

List the common problems of the elderly revealed by Age Concern's research.

Providing the solutions

Various medical groups, social services, advisory services, and official organizations are mentioned in the article. Make a list of any six containing at least one from each group, and say what part they play or played in this scheme to help the elderly.

B Language focus

A letter to a relative

You would like an elderly relative to take advantage of the scheme. Write to her, describing a typical day at the centre, and telling her of the facilities offered.

As a group discuss ways in which your letters would have to be changed if you were trying to dissuade her from spending time with what in your opinion were a group of people too old to be interesting.

Which ones mean the same?

(a) people who only use the facilities occasionally (paragraph 2)

(b) the scheme cannot operate without help from volunteers (paragraph 5)

(c) the reasons for recommending certain people to use the services (paragraph 6)

Find the phrases in the article that mean the same as those listed above, and say why it was more appropriate to use the ones that were used in the article.

To sum up

It is suggested that one of the benefits of fundraising is that it draws attention to the existence of the day centres and makes them better known. What phrase is used to express this effect of publicity fundraising on the centres? (paragraph 4)

One of the main advantages of Age Concern Leominster's scheme is that as it develops, it will need less support by their staff, freeing them to develop other services. What is the term used to express this advantage? (paragraph 8)

Choosing a title

Paragraph 9 makes reference to 'this exciting project'. Do you think the title would lead you to expect anything exciting in the article? What would be your choice of title to reflect the uniqueness of the scheme?

C Discussion

How does the scheme tackle the problem of loneliness among old people? How does it offer relief for carers? What are the advantages to a community of having this kind of service, from the point of view of those who are not yet old? How can a project like this actually help to build up a community spirit?

Job cuts at the Natural History Museum

Background

Cultural pursuits are a minority interest and never attract as much government funding as more pressing social needs. More and more these days, funding has to be attracted from outside sources in the form of sponsorship by industry and large commercial concerns. In a stringent financial climate, job cutting is a way of saving money, as for various reasons, short-term staff are cheaper to employ than long-term staff.

Pre-viewing

What do you suppose will be the attitude of those whose jobs are going to be cut?

What action might they take to show how they feel?

Video

A The main issue

Why are workers on strike at the Natural History Museum?

Facts and figures

What do the following numbers refer to?

- 1,000,000; 100; 109; 1988

B Language focus

Different approaches

Work in pairs to write brief accounts of the televised report to appear in your local newspaper (seventy words). One of you should write a strictly factual account, and the other an account that sympathizes with the Director. Afterwards compare your versions paying particular attention to the type of vocabulary used.

A new image?

The Director talks about making 'some changes', 'new blood', and 'a streamlined museum'. What kind of changes are implied by the use of the word 'new', and how are they related to the concept of a streamlined museum? What overall image of the museum does the Director want to present?

How were they behaving?

Look at the opening section of the report showing the strikers outside the Museum. Describe what you can see, and suggest a reason why the reporter uses the word 'unacademic', and refers to 'antics' rather than 'behaviour' or 'conduct'.

Ways of putting in money

BP is short for British Petroleum, an oil company. Why do you think the reporter says they are '**pumping** in £1 million' in preference to '**donating** £1 million'?

C Discussion

Describe the sort of things you would find in a natural history museum. What are your views on sponsorship? How do you think museums should be funded?

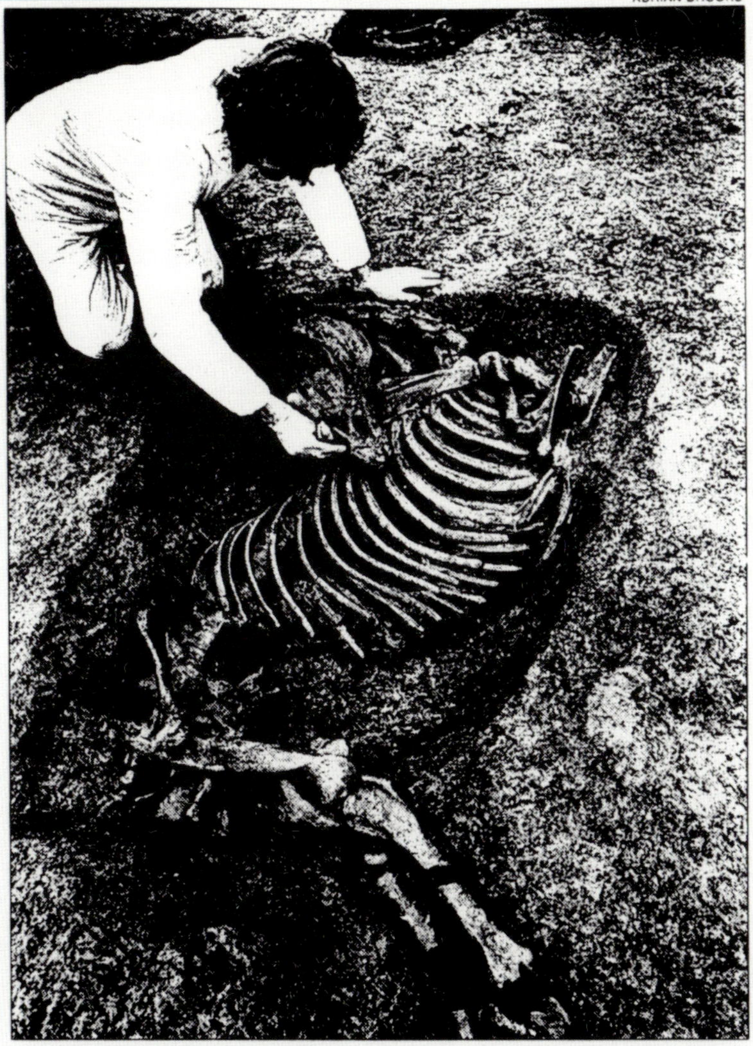

Bones of history: an archaeologist clearing soil from the skeleton of the Iron Age horse at Stratford. Human bones were found in a smaller ditch nearby

Tube dig finds Iron Age bones

By Michael Dynes, Transport Correspondent

SKELETONS of a human and a horse which archaeologists believe may have been sacrificial victims have been found in an Iron Age grave unearthed in excavations for London Underground's proposed Jubilee Line extension.

The skeletons were found lying at either end of a semicircular burial chamber, 4ft below the surface, near the Lea river in Stratford, east London.

The grave has been dated to around 300 BC, and is being seen as one of the most significant Iron Age discoveries in the London area.

Iron Age man was of Celtic extraction, and spoke a language similar to Welsh. Throughout the period, horses were regarded as sacred and their skulls were sometimes placed as offerings at the entrances to fortifications.

The discovery of a man alongside a horse has, however, raised the possibility that both were killed as part of a religious ritual.

John Dillon, an archaeologist from the British Museum seconded to the Jubilee Line excavation team, said that few Iron Age cemeteries had been found.

"Evidence from other sites suggests that after death, human bodies were dismembered, possibly as part of a ritual offering to a deity," he said.

Because of their place in society, people often were given the special treatment of being buried whole. The alternative was that they might have been a human sacrifice, he added.

David Wilkinson, an archaeologist from the Oxford Archaeological Unit, which is excavating the site, said: "This discovery is something special.

"The horse is likely to have been sacrificed for religious reasons. Sacrifice is a possible explanation for the remaining skeleton, although with limited direct evidence it is difficult to be sure."

London was established as a city by the Romans who conquered the local inhabitants, during which time the need for communications to the continent up the Thames and along the Lea Valley would have made Stratford more important than the capital.

☐ The remains of an Anglo-Saxon prince buried with his horse have been discovered at the Sutton Hoo burial ground at Woodbridge, Suffolk.

They are the first contents of a burial mound at the riverside site to be found intact by archaeologists since the great ship burial was unearthed in 1939.

The Times – 28 November 1991

Tube dig finds Iron Age bones

A True or false?

1 The skeletons were found in a burial chamber.

2 The burial chamber was square in shape.

3 The grave has been dated to around 500 BC.

4 The skeletons are of a human and a horse.

5 Archaeologists think the bones may be those of sacrificial victims.

B Language focus

You were there

You are very keen on archaeology and were there when the grave was discovered. Write to a friend who shares your enthusiasm, giving all the details. First of all though, discuss as a group why the use of the passive might not be appropriate here.

Why the passive?

Look at the following sentences, all taken from the article, and, from what you have learnt from the writing exercise above, give reasons why the passive was used so often in the article.

(a) Skeletons have been found in an Iron Age grave.
(b) The grave has been dated to around 300 BC.
(c) Throughout the period horses were regarded as sacred.
(d) Few Iron Age cemeteries have been found.

Comparing the versions

Compare your version of the facts with that of the article. Apart from the change of voice from active to passive, what other differences can you note?

In summary

The title of the article is in effect a five-word summary of the first paragraph. Make a note of the linguistic changes that have been made to achieve this reduction.

C Discussion

Apart from human and animal remains, what sort of other things are found in digs? What is the value of archaeology? If you were going to take part in a dig, which part of the world would you like it to be in, and what would you like to find?

British Studies: facts and figures about the elderly

Old age is causing increasing problems both for the individual who is growing older, and the State which has to make provision for its elderly population. Below are some facts and figures about the elderly from a fact sheet published by the Family Policy Studies Centre, which was established in 1983 as a successor to the Study Commission on the Family. The Centre is an independent body, free of any political affiliation and has no collective policies.

The 'young elderly' and the 'old elderly'

It makes little sense to describe everyone over the age of sixty or sixty-five as 'the elderly population', or 'old people'. Old age can cover a period often of thirty to thirty-five years or more; those just entering their retirement will be a generation younger than some of the oldest citizens. A distinction is often made between the 'young elderly' – aged sixty-five to seventy-four – and the 'old elderly' – those aged seventy-five+ or eighty-five+. Apart from the fact that these two main groups differ from each other in terms of physical, social and economic characteristics, the distinction is important because of the changing balance in the composition of the elderly population overall.

Table D: percentage of the population aged 65+ 1901–2041 Great Britain

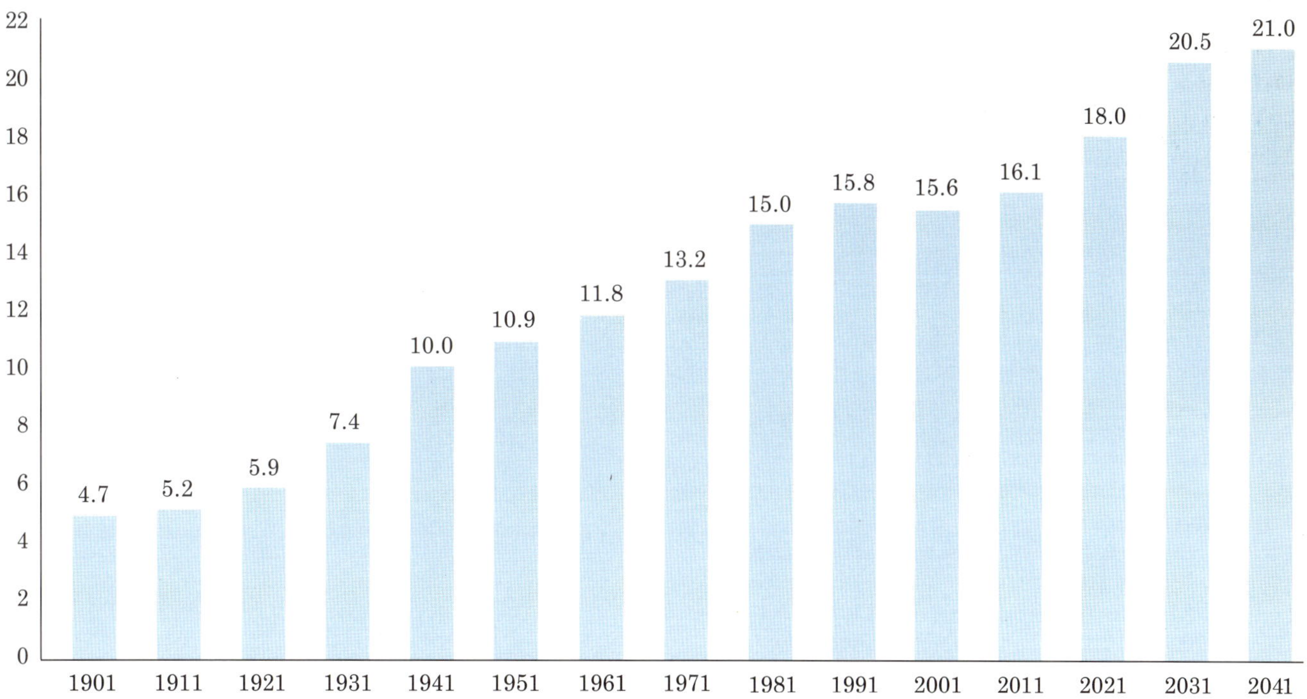

The Family Policy Studies Centre

Sources: OPCS census data 1901–1981
Population projections by the Government Actuary 1987–2027
OPCS PP2 No. 16

Centenarians

The survival of more people to a very old age is clear if centenarians are considered. While a 100th birthday is still unusual, the Royal congratulatory telegram is not the rarity it once was.

Table E: numbers of centenarians

1951	**1961**	**1971**	**1981**
271	479	1,240	2,410

Source: OPCS Population Trends 38 Winter 1984

The present number of centenarians will not be known until the publication of the 1991 census.

Over to you

In the classroom

1 Apart from the fact that people are living longer, can you think of any other reason why the percentage of old people in the population is growing?

2 What do you consider to be the advantages of the 'young elderly' as opposed to the 'old elderly' from the point of view of (a) health and (b) finance? Suggest some positive aspects to ageing, and the contribution old people make to society.

3 Look at Table E and estimate the 1991 number of centenarians, and then make a projection for the year 2041.

An outside project

1 Try to find some statistical information from your own country on the following:

(a) The number of elderly people as a percentage of the population.
(b) Where the elderly are cared for, e.g. at home or in 'old people's homes'.
(c) The relationship between old age and disability.

2 Each person in the group is to interview four people aged sixty, two male and two female, with the intention of finding out their attitudes to approaching old age. As a group, work out a standard set of eight questions and, after the interviews, pool your information and try to produce a statistical report from the answers received:

e.g. seventy per cent looked forward to having more leisure time.

Heathrow runways

Background

Air travel has increased dramatically over recent years, and passenger numbers are expected to double between now and the year 2000. Heathrow, London's main airport, is seriously short of runway space and needs to expand if it is not to lose traffic to other international airports.

Note: MPs stands for Members of Parliament; CAA stands for Civil Aviation Authority.

Pre-viewing

In this report, commercial interests are pressing for permission to fly more planes from Heathrow. Can you think of a group of people who might want to oppose this development?

Video

A The main issues

1 What are British Midland's plans for Heathrow?

2 Why are local residents against these plans?

3 What are the MP's views?

B Language focus

Profits or peace of mind?

Both sides of the dispute are submitting their arguments to the Minister in the form of a letter containing four main points. Work in pairs, with one of you writing from the point of view of British Midland, and the other from that of the residents. Compare your versions to see how they differ in style, highlighting the linguistic features that reflect the difference. (seventy words)

How bad is the situation?

'Britain is already chronically short of airport capacity.'

'Chronic' is a word used in connection with serious illness.

What is being implied by its use here, with reference to the future of Heathrow as a major international airport?

Words betray the heart

Compare the following sets of vocabulary:

- vital national asset, hub airport, develop vigorously, full potential (paragraph 3)
- shopping, visit friends, gardening, sit at home, peace of mind (paragraph 9)

What sort of real-life contexts are suggested by these words, and how does this choice of vocabulary reflect the opposing attitudes of the speakers?

What did it say in the report?

Pick out the words that are used in the report instead of the proposed alternatives printed in bold below:

(a) Residents in Longford and Hatton have a **temporary break** from the noise until 3 o'clock. (paragraph 2)
(b) All areas would be subject to **continual** daytime noise. (paragraph 2)
(c) Heathrow is an **essential** national asset. (paragraph 3)

What additional element of meaning is present in the word the reporter chose to use that is absent from 'temporary break' used in (a) above?

C Role play

Work in pairs: one of you is the Chairman of British Midland, the other lives near Heathrow. What would each of you say to persuade the other to accept your point of view?

British Midland to challenge BA

Daniel John, Transport Correspondent

British Midland is to axe one of its loss-making domestic routes to free space at Heathrow airport for the launch of its new service to Brussels in competition with British Airways and Sabena, the Belgian carrier.

The five-flights-a-day link to Liverpool will close on March 28 to allow BM to start operating the Brussels route the following day as part of the airline's effort to expand its European network.

Sir Michael Bishop, BM's chairman, said the Brussels route was a major step forward in its plan to challenge national flag carriers which hold a duopoly on at least nine major European destinations.

BM plans to undercut BA and Sabena on fares to Brussels by nearly 30 per cent. It intends to charge a business fare of £190 return, compared with the £290 of its two competitors, and run six daily flights.

But the ending of services to Liverpool will raise fears in the regions that their links with London are at risk to new business being generated on the Continent.

BM, which is Britain's second biggest short-haul airline, yesterday emphasised that its commitment to serving UK cities remained as strong as ever.

It pointed to the launch of a new route to Frankfurt from East Midlands Airport as a sign of its regional strength.

However, BM has made no secret of its plans to serve the German city from Heathrow, a move currently prevented by the lack of take-off and landing slots at the London airport.

Failure to secure more slots could result in BM using some of its flight times allotted to East Midlands and Birmingham airports to get the Heathrow service off the ground later this year.

The announcement of the new Brussels route came as BM revealed it had returned to profit after losses of nearly £12 million in 1990. Pre-tax profits of £2.5 million for 1991 were struck, despite one of the worst years in aviation history.

BM saw its revenues climb from £197 million to £223 million, which reflected a 7 per cent increase in the number of passengers carried to just over 4 million. The airline cut staff by 10 per cent to 2,900.

Its routes to Paris and Dublin, which incurred high development costs in 1990, made a profit. BM expects its growing European network to contribute about 45 per cent of its revenue over the year, up from 29 per cent in 1990 and 37 per cent in 1991.

The company's performance should see its parent, Airlines of Britain, turn in a similar profit figure. Sir Michael said the other operating arms of the group, Manx Airlines, which is making money, and Loganair, the small Scottish and Northern Ireland carrier which is losing cash, would cancel each other out.

The Guardian – 25 February 1992

British Midland to challenge BA

A Facts...

How will British Midland's plans for expanding its European network affect its existing service?

...and figures

What do the following refer to?

- 30%; £190; £290; 7%; 2,900; 45%

B Language focus

The current state of affairs

Write a factual statement detailing British Midland's present financial position and future plans and expectations. (seventy words)

Give the same information, this time in a positive report for the shareholders. What linguistic features will be present in the second and absent from the first?

Putting it differently

(a) British Midland emphasized its commitment to serving UK cities.
(b) British Midland emphasized that it is committed to serving UK cities.

Suggest a context in which (a) might be more appropriate than (b).

(a) It is the intention of British Midland to expand its services.
(b) British Midland intends to expand its services.

Which of the above would you use if you wanted to focus on what you intended to do, rather than your intention to do it?

Choosing words carefully

- 'to axe' or 'to cut'

What ideas are suggested by 'axe', that are absent in 'cut'?

Why do you think the reporter preferred 'axe' to 'cut' in this particular context?

Something to suit the occasion

- a major step forward
- great progress
- a significant advance

Say which of the above you would use in the following contexts:

(a) a scientific paper commenting on the effect of a new discovery
(b) a school report referring to a child's improvement in a subject
(c) a conversation referring to the invention of the wheel
(d) a campaign speech by a politician about his party's plans to introduce new benefits for old people
(e) a written or spoken context wanting to make a statement that things have moved forward without being too specific

Note: in some contexts, more than one of the expressions listed will be appropriate.

C Your turn

You are trying to persuade your grandmother to travel by air for the first time, and think it would be a good idea to stress the aspects of comfort, convenience, and expense. What will you say to her?

Villagers and speeding traffic

Background

Road numbers preceded by the letter 'M' are motorways. The M25, a circular road running round London, is one of the busiest motorways in Britain.

'A' roads are the major trunk roads between towns and cities; 'B' roads are the minor county roads.

'Road-hog' is the name given to a selfish or reckless motorist who drives without concern for other road users.

Pre-viewing

1 Who else might you expect to be involved in this report apart from the villagers and the speeding motorists?

2 Why might motorists speeding through a village be more dangerous there than in other places?

3 Suggest two scenes you might expect to see in this report.

Video

A Traffic problems

1 Why have the residents of Theydon Bois bought a speed gun?

2 What specific problems do they have with the speeding traffic?

3 Who have they asked for help with the problem?

B Language focus

The voice of officialdom

You disagree with the sentiments expressed in paragraph 5 of the transcript. Write a brief response to the Council representative's argument saying why you think immediate action is necessary. (sixty words)

Compare your response with his statement and say what main differences you notice in the type of language used. In what ways is yours more colourful or forceful?

Taking it personally

Below is an alternative version of the Council representative's report:

There are 2,000 places within Essex where there is a worse accident record. Now it is surely right that the places where people are actually being injured should be dealt with, rather than where they might be, regrettable though that may be.

Compare the above version with the original and say what effect is created by the use of the personal pronoun?

Putting ideas into your head

(a) hundreds of cars and lorries thunder down this little road (paragraph 2)
(b) lots of traffic races down the little road

(a) before tragedy strikes (paragraph 8)
(b) before there is an accident

Above are expressions used by the reporter, followed by a possible alternative. What ideas was the reporter wanting to stress in each case that made (a) more appropriate than (b)?

Changing it round

The first sentence in paragraph 3 of the transcript was originally spoken. Suggest ways in which it could be changed to become suitable as a written text.

C Role play

Work in pairs, and choose a role in one of the following situations:

(a) the parent of a child injured by a speeding motorist
a television interviewer
(b) a police officer
a driver stopped for exceeding the speed limit
(c) a villager complaining about speeding motorists
a council representative

400 caught already in bid to cut death and injury on roads

No hiding place as cameras trap speeding drivers

by **Sarah Edwards**

More than 400 speeding drivers have been trapped by a spy camera in the centre of Oxford and thousands more across the county are now facing prosecution unless they keep to the speed limit.

A £300,000 system of cameras designed to cut the number of accidents causing injury on Oxfordshire's roads is about to go live after extensive trials.

Thames Valley Police revealed this week that a camera at traffic lights in Thames Street, Oxford had trapped hundreds of motorists.

Its operation in conjunction with Oxfordshire County Council will now be stepped up as a ring of spy cameras comes into action the length and breadth of the county. Motorists have already become familiar with the speed camera warning signs.

Chief Superintendent Peter Vinar, the head of the Thames Valley Police Traffic Department, told *The Oxford Times*: "I hope that speeding will become as socially unacceptable as is drink driving.

"Some cameras are already working. We have had the equipment since April and we have been evaluating the system.

"We are already starting to notice a fall in overall speeds, which is very encouraging."

According to police statistics, serious road accidents and deaths are costing the community £185 million every year.

Chief Superintendent Vinar added: "Our research shows that speed is the largest single factor which causes accidents. More than one third of all accidents are caused by speed."

By the end of 1994 there will be 30 strategically placed cameras in Oxfordshire photographing speeding vehicles 24 hours a day.

Some will be fixed at accident black spots but others are mobile and can be moved around the county by police officers.

A computer system linked to the central ticket office and the magistrates court will administer a system of fixed £40 penalty fines and three penalty points.

However, drivers who are caught exceeding the speed limit by more than 25 miles an hour will face automatic court appearances, and heavier penalties.

The Oxford Times – 4 June 1993

No hiding place as cameras trap speeding drivers

A Setting the trap?

1 State the purpose of the installation of the speed cameras.

2 Explain why it is necessary to make sure that speed limits are observed.

B Language focus

Socially unacceptable?

Write an information sheet about speeding to be used by the police in a campaign designed to persuade people that speeding is unacceptable. What will you say to try to change the public image of the speed cameras, and how will you say it? What linguistic features will you definitely exclude?

Recording or spying?

Wherever speed cameras are in operation there is a warning sign informing motorists of their presence. The reporter however, twice refers to 'spy' cameras, and talks about motorists being 'trapped'. What popular attitude towards the use of the cameras by the police does this reveal?

Examining the headlines

Look at the headlines of the article, both the smaller one, which is underlined, and the main one. Give a reason why the words below on the left were used rather than their synonyms on the right:

• bid	attempt
• cut	reduce
• drivers	motorists

Make a list of the other linguistic features that are typical of headline writing.

Why one rather than the other?

(a) go live (paragraph 2)
come into effect

(b) accident black spots (paragraph 11) places where lots of accidents have happened

(c) the length and breadth of the county (paragraph 4)
all over the county

Why do you think the first expressions were used in preference to those below?

C Discussion

Do you agree with the use of speed cameras or do you think it a form of spying? Can you think of any other method of making sure that motorists obey speed limits? What are the advantages to the police of using speed cameras? Why do you think people find speeding more socially acceptable than drink driving? How are motorists in your country prevented from speeding?

British Studies: transport statistics

Below are two sets of transport statistics. The first deals with car ownership, and the second with the types of road user involved in fatal and serious road accidents. You will see that drivers of cars feature largely in this section. The statistics, which were originally published by the Department of Transport, were reproduced from *Regional trends 27* Crown copyright 1992 and *Social trends 23* Crown copyright 1993.

Table F: cars[1] and car ownership: by region, 1981 and 1990

Percentages and cars per 1,000 population

United Kingdom	1981 Percentage of households without the regular use of a car	1981 Percentage of households with regular use of: One car only	1981 Percentage of households with regular use of: Two or more cars	1981 Cars per 1,000 pop.	1990 Percentage of households without the regular use of a car	1990 Percentage of households with regular use of: One car only	1990 Percentage of households with regular use of: Two or more cars	1990 Cars per 1,000 pop.
Great Britain	40	45	15	281	33	44	23	363
North	48	41	10	227	42	43	16	295
Yorkshire and Humberside	46	43	12	245	38	46	16	323
East Midlands	37	47	15	273	31	44	24	351
East Anglia	31	51	18	321	26	47	26	420
South-East	36	46	19	316	28	44	28	396
Greater London	45	42	14	287	38	42	19	355
Rest of South East	30	48	22	336	23	45	32	420
South-West	31	51	18	329	25	48	27	410
West Midlands	38	46	16	290	35	42	24	386
North-West	45	42	13	250	37	44	20	338
England	39	45	16	288	32	44	23	372
Wales	38	47	15	271	30	49	21	346
Scotland	49	40	11	217	42	41	17	294
Northern Ireland	40	46	14	237	34	47	19	302

[1] Includes cars and vans normally available to the household.

Source: Department of Transport

Table G: road accidents, vehicles involved and casualties – *Great Britain*

Number

Killed and seriously injured		1981	1982	1983	1984	1985	1986	1987	1988	1989	1990	1991
By type of road user												
Child pedestrians	KKLJ	6547	6695	6640	6823	6663	5992	5472	5471	5437	5545	4790
Adult pedestrians	KKLK	11817	12169	12139	12638	12576	12880	11978	12207	11859	11597	10032
Child pedal cyclists	KKLL	2096	2058	2287	2269	1704	1396	1458	1322	1370	1295	1200
Adult pedal cyclists	KKLM	3393	3893	4109	4326	3910	3814	3638	3526	3730	3270	2945
Moped riders	KKLN	2903	3109	3241	3188	2919	2571	2221	1903	1729	1417	989
Motor scooter riders	KKLO	515	608	647	748	715	606	499	380	382	289	226
Motor scooter passengers	KCUU	62	106	95	100	93	66	71	46	44	24	20
Motor cycle riders	KCUV	16398	16296	14260	14109	12838	11819	9989	9364	9414	8576	6600
Motor cycle passengers	KCUW	2400	2514	2021	1805	1547	1370	1086	924	884	783	651
Car and taxi drivers	KCUX	19149	19460	15472	16530	16722	17132	17167	17576	17834	17403	15629
Car and taxi passengers	KCUY	14476	14525	11574	12467	12385	12554	11919	11770	11850	11717	9764
Users of buses and coaches	KCUZ	961	962	969	929	1036	859	892	912	835	807	725
Users of goods vehicles	KCVA	2891	2797	2283	2354	2454	2552	2637	2485	2673	2399	2122
Users of other vehicles	KCVB	308	312	278	313	254	263	229	255	247	251	229

Over to you

In the classroom

1 Which area of England had the largest percentage increase in the number of households with two cars over the period covered?

2 Which country in Britain had the highest percentage drop in the number of households without regular use of a car?

3 Which were the peak years for road accidents in all categories of road user?

4 What has been the general trend over the last ten years?

5 Given that there are now more cars on the road, how would you account for the difference between the 1981 and the 1991 figures for serious accidents caused to car and taxi drivers and their passengers?

An outside project

Work in pairs for tasks 1 and 2, and then as a group for the remaining tasks.

1 Interview thirty people to find out how many times per week they use the following: car, bus, train, bicycle.

2 Work out which is the most popular form of transport for your own particular sample, and then compare findings with other pairs.

3 For each of the last five years, collect data on the number of cars on the road, and fatal road accidents to pedestrians involving cars.

4 See if there is any correlation between the number of cars and the number of fatal accidents.

5 Suggest a series of measures that could be taken to reduce all types of road accident.

Women priests

Background

At the time of this report, the Church of England was in the process of deciding whether to ordain women to the priesthood. The question was first debated and voted on at local level, but the final decision had to be made by the General Synod, the highest governing body in the Church, consisting of representatives of the bishops, the clergy, and the laity.

Pre-viewing

In order to give a balanced view of the argument, how many people do you think should be interviewed? How would you divide them between clergy and laity, men and women?

Video

A Setting the scene

1 State four items of information given about Rochester.

2 Give the occupations of the three people interviewed.

B Language focus

Pros and cons

Summarize the arguments presented for the ordination of women by the woman deacon from the point of view of an outsider. Then, write an outline of her argument from the point of view of someone opposed to it.

Compare your versions, and see what changes in style you have made in moving from one to the other.

High feeling?

The presenter says 'feelings are already running high', and the reporter talks about people being 'vehement'. Are there in fact any indications of anger or aggressiveness in the text? Make a note of the opening words of each the three interviewees and say what approach to the subject they suggest. If feelings are high, why doesn't it show?

Who thought it?

The last paragraph of the transcript begins: 'It's thought that ...'. Give a reason why the passive is used here, and suggest an alternative in the active.

Putting like with like

From the words listed below, pick out three clusters with similar meanings:

- issue, think, vehement, believe, matter, passionate, hold, consider, forceful, topic, subject, heated, theme, intense

C Discussion

In the video the bishop refers to the question of power. Do you think the argument about women priests is really about power, or do other considerations play a part? What qualities do you think women could bring to the priesthood?

Home News

Bishops meet in secret to discuss Anglican crisis

The House of Bishops of the Church of England met from Monday to Thursday of this week in Manchester, at an undisclosed location and with a confidential agenda. It was anticipated that they would issue a statement towards the end of the week that would be "carefully timed to miss everybody's deadlines", suggested Steve Jenkins, press officer at Church House. However, it was known that the continuing crisis over women priests would be discussed, as well as theological training.

It is understood that the group of 13 bishops who voted against the legislation (there was also one abstention) met beforehand so that they could go to Manchester united behind a single proposal. It is also understood that the Archbishop of York, Dr John Habgood, has been acting as unofficial mediator with these bishops. It is not yet known what their proposal has been, but a number of possibilities have been raised.

At the simplest level there could be a continuation of the existing practice whereby **bishops from neighbouring dioceses can help each other out** with confirmations or even ordinations. And so a bishop opposed to women priests, who had "kept his hands clean", could minister to clergy and laity opposed to women priests in other dioceses, at the invitation of their diocesan bishop. And, vice versa, a bishop with "clean hands" could still have women priests in his diocese if they had been ordained by someone else. One bishop said before the meeting that "the buzz" was that this would be the decision, and it would require no legal formalities.

A next step up from that would be a more organised system of **"flying bishops"**. Such a scheme would begin to look more like a parallel Church. But for many conservative Anglicans this scheme would not go far enough, because flying bishops would still be answerable to the General Synod and to the archbishops of Canterbury or York – whose authority for them has now been called into question.

At a further level above that would be a **"third province"**, which would be non-territorial – the first two provinces being Canterbury and York. This proposal has been formalised by a small group of seven people, including two evangelicals, who explain in their statement: "The third province could be separate from the Church of England (like all the other provinces in the Anglican Communion) or it could form part of the established Church, but either way it must be self-governing, with its own archbishop, its own canon law and a fair share of the buildings and other assets". William Bridge, one of the seven proposers of the scheme, explained that it was preferable to the flying bishops scheme because of its completely separate authority structure: "We have no confidence at all either in the two archbishops or the bishops who voted for the liberal Church", he said. "We want a complete break with the whole lot."

The umbrella group for Anglo-Catholics opposed to women priests, **Forward in Faith**, is not endorsing any of those schemes, and indeed doubts if any of them go far enough."I cannot understand how you can have a third province when you have a difficulty with the first two", explained Michael Barwick, their director, and he described the "flying bishops" proposal as "a strange idea", because diocesan bishops would not want other bishops interfering in their dioceses. As far as Forward in Faith was concerned, the bottom line was a **"guaranteed succession"**, he said, of orders and sacraments rather than a scheme that would last only for the lifetime of the traditionalists: "we are not in this for something that will keep us happy, without giving anything to our children and grandchildren".

Bishops meet in secret to discuss Anglican crisis

Behind closed doors

1 Explain why you think the bishops met in secret, and whose 'deadlines' they wanted to miss.

2 State what you think is meant by the expression 'clean hands' in this context.

B Language focus

Something for future generations

What point does the Forward in Faith group want to stress by referring to 'our children and grandchildren'? Give a reason why this phrase was used instead of 'future generations'. What attitude to faith does it imply?

Active or passive?

• it was anticipated	(paragraph 1)
• it was known	(paragraph 1)
• it is understood	(paragraph 2)
• it is not yet known	(paragraph 2)

Suggest possible alternatives in the active for the above, using a pronoun or a noun. Then say why you think the passive was preferred.

A secret meeting

Pick out three phrases in the first paragraph that stress the aspect of secrecy. What is the verb used that suggests probability rather than certainty about future events?

Making a break

1 We want a complete break with the whole lot.

2 We want a complete break with all of them.

What does the use of the first expression suggest to you about the attitude of the speaker towards his opponents?

C Discussion

The video report was made before the decision to ordain women to the priesthood, and the article was written afterwards. Did the video prepare you for the situation described in the article? What is the status of women in your country as regards religion? Do they take part in religious services? Do they occupy positions of leadership in religious contexts? Do you think the existing situation as regards women is likely to change in the future?

Christ and Christmas

Background

For several years Christians have been concerned that the feast of Christmas has become an excuse for aggressive commercialism, rather than for celebrating the birthday of Christ. In recent years they have tried to reverse the trend, and Christians of all denominations are working together to make people think again about Christmas and put Christ back at the centre of the celebration.

Note: Peter Pan – the main character in a play for children of the same name by J.M.Barrie.

The Tooth Fairy – when young children lose a tooth, there is a custom of hiding the tooth supposedly for a fairy to find and leave some money in exchange for the tooth.

Pre-viewing

1 Discuss what Christmas means for members of the group. Is it associated with any particular memories?

2 Is Christmas more important for children than for adults?

3 Suggest two scenes you might expect to see in a video about Christmas.

Video

A The real meaning of Christmas

What is the purpose of the Christmas Unwrapped campaign?

The popular view

1 Summarize the attitudes of the people interviewed in the street about Christmas.

2 Which was the most disturbing poll result for the churches?

B Language focus

A publicity poster

You are designing a poster to accompany the campaign, and only have space for twenty words. Which ones will you choose to encapsulate the message you are trying to put across? What sort of grammatical choices will the lack of space force upon you?

Only thirty-three shopping days left...

What attitudes to Christmas are implied by calculating the period of time leading to Christmas in terms of shopping days. Can you suggest a phrase that the churches could use as an alternative?

Fighting talk

The word 'campaign' suggests a military operation. Pick out the vocabulary in paragraphs 2 and 10 that supports this view.

Choosing a good slogan

Below are some alternative slogans for the campaign. Compare them with the original and say what it is that makes a good campaign slogan.

(a) the real meaning of Christmas
(b) the best present of all
(c) Christmas without commercialism
(d) Christmas repackaged

C Speaking for yourself

What is the most important religious holiday in your country? Is it also the most popular one? Explain its significance and describe how that day or the most popular religious festival would be celebrated.

Boycott Turkey Meat

Chickens' Lib has been calling for a boycott of turkeys since 1989 to protest against the inhumane way in which they are reared and slaughtered. As most turkeys are sold at Christmas, co-founder, Clare Druce, outlines the reason for the boycott.

Until the turkey industry cleans up its act, turkey meat should be off the menu of any ethical consumer. (A growing number of people are questioning whether these sensitive and beautiful birds should be eaten at all, but that's another area of debate.) Even the most confirmed carnivore/Christmas turkey-eater might be willing to join our boycott once the full story is told. It's a sad, sad story of greed and cruel exploitation and not much to do with farming as most people would like to understand it. And it's deeply ironic that in the season of goodwill so many families give pride of place to the end product of misery and terror.

Breeding

In its wild state, the turkey can fly at speeds of up to 50mph, yet the modern male farmed variety is now not only earth-bound, but also too broad breasted to mate naturally, following 'progress' in breading a meatier bird. Never mind! Artificial Insemination (AI) is there to save the day and to ensure maximum hatchability and profits. AI? Isn't that just a modern procedure and quite acceptable? We don't think so.

AI involves a team of operators 'milking' the breeding males two or three times a week for their semen, stimulating the genital area until an erection is achieved and the semen ejected – a kind of human-to-bird masturbation. The stress endured by these sensitive and nervous creatures has never been investigated, but can be imagined. Then the females must be inseminated, by having a length of tubing inserted into the vagina. Two or three operators are required to achieve this apology for the real thing.

Once the parent stock have passed their peak of semen-giving and egg-laying, they are slaughtered, and processed into pies, sausages etc. The mature stag weighs the same as an 8–9 year-old child, yet is hung upside down in shackles for up to six minutes, before being electrically stunned. A huge percentage of adult birds suffer from diseases of the hip joints. The pain of the shackles can be guessed at. That is the background to the turkey industry, for it all begins with the parent stock.

Housing

In 1991 something approaching 40 million turkeys will have been reared and slaughtered. There are two main systems of turkey rearing: windowless units similar to broiler sheds (larger ones housing around 15,000 birds) and 'pole barns', which are naturally lit and vent-ilated. In both systems, the stocking density is very tight, and by the time the birds reach slaughter age (between 12 and 26 weeks – their natural lifespan being 10 years) they are thick on the ground. In the windowless units, the sheds are dimly-lit, and the environment totally controlled. Because lighting intensity can be extremely low to minimise aggression, debeaking is less common under this system. (The Ministry of Agriculture gave Chickens' Lib the figure of 75–80% for turkeys suffering the mutilation of debeaking, but the British Turkey Federation is contesting this.) In pole barns, most (perhaps all) birds are debeaked, because aggression is inevitable in the crowded and naturally-lit environment.

So the 'choice' is between the squalor of the sheds or the chronic pain and depression endured by debeaked poultry. Mortality runs at around 7%, though much higher figures are quoted. Much of the loss occurs early on in the young birds' lives, when some fail to find the food and water points. These non-profit making poults are known in the industry as 'starve-outs'. Foot and leg problems abound, wet litter causing ulcerated feet and hock burns in badly-run units. Aggression in the stressed birds can lead to terrible injuries, especially to the eyes. Veterinary Record (12/10/91) carried this depressing report on the health status of turkeys:

"The seasonal increase in submissions (to Veterinary Investigation Centres) from turkeys being reared for the Christmas trade was evident at most centres. The common managemental problems of starvation, water deprivation and heat stress were all frequently diagnosed together with colisepticaemia and yolk sac infections."

Free Range Turkeys

For those who remain convinced that Christmas wouldn't be Christmas without 'the bird', please consider buying a free-range turkey. Poultry from The Real Meat Company is guaranteed free of additives and will have been reared with very high welfare standards right up to and including slaughter. However, even this excellent company relies on poults which are the end-product of artificial insemination. We hope that by next year the Real Meat Company will have tracked down a source of naturally inseminated birds. Other companies produce a small proportion of free range turkeys. 'Farmers Glory' are experimenting with truly free range birds, seemingly living in ideal conditions in a Forestry Commission forest in North Yorkshire. Unfortunately, a proposed visit by Chickens' Lib in late October was cancelled at the last minute, but we hope to see the forest turkeys next year. Not all 'Farmers Glory' free-range birds are from the forest but most are, so this is a label to look out for. We at Chickens' Lib are dedicated to raising public consciousness about the cruelty behind the British Christmas dinner. We sincerely hope that all who read this magazine will put ethics before tradition.

The Ethical Consumer – December 1991 /January 1992

Boycott turkey meat

A A merry Christmas?

1 In what ways is the modern male farmed turkey different from a turkey in the wild state?

2 Describe the turkeys' housing conditions.

B Language focus

What are your views now?

Has the article changed your understanding of the term 'factory farming'? Write down your instinctive reaction to the facts disclosed in the article. Make a list of the number and type of adjectives you have used and then check with a partner to see how your versions compare.

Making a point with punctuation

In paragraph 2 of the article the writer uses a variety of punctuation apart from the usual full stops and commas. What point is she trying to make by placing 'progress' in inverted commas; what is the purpose of the exclamation mark; and do the question marks indicate real questions?

Why mention it?

The stress ...... can be imagined. (paragraph 3)
The pain ...... can be guessed at. (paragraph 4)

Why do you think the writer mentions these things for which she has no statistical evidence, when her article is based on facts and figures which can be verified?

Choosing the right expression

(a) they are thick on the ground (paragraph 5)
(b) there are lots of them

What was the particular context referred to that made (a) more appropriate than (b)?

(a) cleans up its act (paragraph 1)
(b) puts its house in order
(c) stamps out abuses
(d) changes its practices

Which of the above expressions do you think best suggests all the changes that the turkey industry needs to make?

C Discussion

Do you think the general public realises just what is involved in factory farming? After reading this article, would you support the boycott? Do you think legal action should be taken against factory farmers? What part do you think the RSPCA (the Royal Society for the Prevention of Cruelty to Animals) could play? Is there much factory farming in your country?

British Studies: religious life in Britain

Below are some facts and figures about religious life in Britain taken from a book entitled Religion, published by Her Majesty's Stationery Office in the Aspects of Britain series.

(a) Everyone in Britain has the right to religious freedom (in teaching, worship and observance) without interference from the community or the State. Religious organizations and groups may own property, run schools, and promote their beliefs in speech and writing.

(b) Britain has a long tradition of religious tolerance, and the past thirty years have seen the acceptance of the wide variety of religious beliefs and traditions of the large numbers of immigrants of different nationalities, although immigrants also belong to Britain's existing Christian denominations.

(c) Recent surveys suggest that about ten per cent of the adult population of Britain regularly attend church.

(d) According to the results of one survey, published in 1991, fifty-four per cent of the population of Britain claimed to be religious and seventy-one per cent said they believe in God. Twenty-five per cent retained a Christian belief in hell and forty-four per cent said they believed in life after death. Sixty-five percent said it was important to have a religious service following the birth of a child, seventy-nine per cent said it was important for a marriage and eighty-four per cent for a death.

Her Majesty's Stationery Office

Over to you

In the classroom

1 How do you account for the fact that although fifty-four per cent of the population claim to be religious, only ten per cent of adults regularly attend church?

2 Give reasons why you think people find it important to have religious services connected with birth, marriage and death.

3 How far do you think religious intolerance has contributed to the situation in Northern Ireland, or do you think the problem is political rather than religious?

An outside project

Find out the answers to the following questions about your own country:

1 What is the relationship between the state and religion?

2 How many different religions do you know of that are represented in your country?

3 Do all religions have equal status?

4 Are religions allowed the freedoms listed in (a) above?

5 Are birth, marriage, and death singled out as times of special religious significance?

6 Are people from different religious groupings spread evenly among the population, or do people of the same religion tend to live near each other? Indicate on a map of your area, where different religious groupings live.

Blind people and art

Background

In Britain nearly one million people are blind or partially sighted; almost one person in sixty.

The Tate Gallery is a national gallery of British art in central London. It was opened in 1897 and built at the expense of (Sir) Henry Tate, a sugar manufacturer. In the twentieth century modern foreign paintings and sculpture (both British and foreign) were added.

Pre-viewing

1 What connection between blindness and art does the title of the report suggest to you?

2 Can you think of two locations where the video might have been filmed?

Video

A The basic idea

Explain the purpose of the collaboration between the Tate Gallery and the Living Paintings Trust?

Finding out more

1 What do the albums consist of, and how many are there?

2 The extract mentions two very famous artists. Give their names, and the names of the pictures referred to in the video.

B Language focus

A journalistic assignment

Work in pairs to write a few words for two different papers about the Tate Gallery's new scheme. One of you is to write an announcement for the 'quality' press under the title 'Seeing by touch', the other a news snippet for the popular press under the title 'Come and have a feel!' (seventy to eighty words). Compare your versions and identify the linguistic features appropriate for the second piece.

An ecstatic reaction

In paragraph 5 of the transcript, Carolyn James gives her reaction to the albums. What expressions does she use to indicate that they have provided her with a renewed opportunity to appreciate art that she had thought would no longer be possible? How can you tell that her words were originally spoken rather than written?

What did she do?

- ventured back to a public gallery
- visited a public gallery again

What ideas are associated with venturing that make the first expression reflect Carolyn's activity more accurately than the second?

And we also thought...

Look at paragraph 11 and pick out the main feature that tells you that this was a spoken rather than a written text. Suggest what the speaker intended to say before he changed his mind.

C Role play

Work in pairs, taking it in turns to be a guide and a blind person. As the guide, describe a picture from a magazine making sure you mention content, colour, size, shape, texture, and anything else relevant. As the blind person, try to get your guide to be as specific as possible, e.g. asking the colour of eyes and hair, whether people look sad or happy, etc. Afterwards, describe how playing these roles has added to your understanding of how to appreciate a picture.

The grocer's lad who invented modern art

The Rockies may crumble, Gibraltar may tumble, and even Impressionist prices at auction are not what they used to be. But then they never really were, once the auctioneer's secret loans, extended credits and the like have been taken into account. Such fluctuations have not affected the feelings of the public at large. The Impressionists are still top of the pops. Far and away the best attended London show in recent times has been the Royal Academy's splendid *Monet in the 90s: The Serial Paintings.*

In no important sense has the Impressionist bubble burst: no one seriously thinks that a few way out of line prices paid (or apparently paid) by those eager to buy publicity rather than art made the Impressionists better, or that their cessation makes them worse. Once the initial strangeness of their idiom wore off (which it did very quickly), the Impressionists have been assured the love of most critics and a massive general public, neither of whom are likely to be art buyers on that scale anyway. For critics the popularity is because they were rebels; for the general public it is because their colours are warm and vibrant, their subjects easy to take and usually rather pretty. Both are partly right, but oversimplify and look for easy answers where there are none.

The most popular artist of them all, Monet, is a case in point. Cezanne's famous dictum about him sticks in the memory, and sometimes in the throat. "Just an eye – but what an eye!" It sounds damning in an age when we want our artists to be verbally intelligent. Monet wrote very few letters of any significance, and as a Grand Old Man he tends to be gnomic on the subject of his own work and the ideas behind it. It is therefore often assumed that Monet had great instincts but no intelligence. Those who seek, on the other hand, to present him now as a great thinker about art tend to be betrayed by lack of material. Though Monet was the friend of literary men, and of eloquent politicians like Clemenceau, and could express himself perfectly clearly in words when he chose, the fact remains that he seldom chose to. Several of the published correspondences are decidedly one-sided: flowing dissertations on every subject under the sun may be the rule from his opposite number, while he replies in brief practical notes or gets his companion and later wife Alice Hoschede to write instead.

John Russell Taylor

THE COLOUR OF TIME
Claude Monet
By Virginia Spate
Thames and Hudson, £38

As the lives of artists go, Monet's was quite interesting. He was brought up in and around a grocer's in Le Havre and seems to have acquired a similar canniness in business matters. As a local child prodigy, he got attention early. His beginnings as a professional artist in Paris were nonetheless fraught with the usual difficulties: lack of money, family mistrust, the neces sity to conceal his first romantic relationship with a model and the birth of their first child, in case a disapproving family should cut off his main means of support. But like most of the Impressionists, he later married the woman, legitimised the son, and became respectable. Although he was to go through difficult periods, he had laid the foundations of bourgeois success, and it is no surprise to discover that he was selling well and living in some style already in his thirties.

His early middle life was complicated by his relationship with the wife of one of his patrons, whose family and (presumably) favours he took over when the husband disappeared into bankruptcy. During the 1880s, the decade in question, he travelled a lot, but settled down to patriarchal life in Giverny and cultivating his garden by the end of that decade, elected early to be the Grand Old Man. It would be a recognisable life-pattern for a solid academic painter, not leaving much room for soul. But it must have been all an elaborate protection for his real obsession, which was the painting of light in a way no one had ever done before.

Virginia Spate rehearses the known facts, but wisely concentrates on the inner life as it is revealed in the paintings, without bothering to force too many explicit connections between the facade and the interior. It is the best way. Monet may well have been secretive as a man, but on canvas he is free to let himself be known. Why should we ask of an artist any more than that?

The Times – 5 November 1992

The grocer's lad who invented modern art

A Art appreciation

Why are the Impressionists popular with:

(a) art critics
(b) the general public?

Fill in the gaps with the correct words

1 Monet's life was quite ....

2 He was brought up in ....

3 During the ...... he travelled a lot.

4 Later he settled down to .... in Giverny.

5 His real obsession was with ....

B Language focus

Biographical details

(a) Summarize the details of Monet's early professional life in Paris in four or five sentences.
(b) You very much disapprove of the artist's early period in Paris. Write four or five sentences that are highly critical of his behaviour.

Compare the grammar and vocabulary of your different summaries, and say in which area they differ most.

What does the title suggest?

What is the author trying to stress by referring to the artist as 'the grocer's lad' rather than 'the grocer's son'?

There's a word for it

Choose the words from the article that correspond to the following definitions:

(a) someone with an extraordinary talent (paragraph 4)
(b) shrewdness in financial dealing (paragraph 4)
(c) the appearance presented from the outside (paragraph 6)

A book review?

The article is in fact a book review as the insert under the author's name makes clear. Only the last paragraph however, makes any specific reference to the book. Suggest other contexts for the article if the last paragraph were to be removed.

C In your own words

You are telling a friend about Monet based on the information given in the article. Give a brief outline of the painter's life using your own words.

If there is a painting that you especially like, or one that has made a deep impression on you, talk about it to the group. Say when and where you first saw it and why it has had such an effect on you.

London ballet company to close

Background

The Arts Council of Great Britain was established in 1946. The function of the Council is to develop and improve knowledge, understanding and practice of the arts, which involves increasing their accessability to the public and advising and co-operating with government departments and other bodies. The Council administers a government grant which, in 1992–93, amounted to £221 million. From April 1994 some structural changes will be introduced resulting in separate councils for England, Scotland and Wales.

Pre-viewing

1 Suggest two reasons why a ballet company might have to close.

2 Name the people you would expect to be interviewed in a report about ballet.

Video

A Facts and figures

1 Who is the patron of the London City Ballet Company?

2 Why is the company having to close?

3 How much money do audiences provide?

4 What is the annual running cost of the company?

5 How much was the Arts Council grant, and what was it for?

B Language focus

Begging letters

Work in pairs to draft letters to the Arts Council asking for a larger grant, and to ballet enthusiasts asking them to contribute to a fundraising scheme. Which of the two will be the more formal, and how will your choice of grammar and vocabulary contribute to the formality?

Why start with 'what'?

Rewrite sentences (a) and (b) on the following model:

The thirteen-year-old ballet company is asking for …… .

What the thirteen year-old ballet company is asking for is …… .

(a) The company's annual costs are £1.7 million.
(b) We are a highly successful touring ballet company.

What difference does starting the sentence with 'what' make?

Whose fault is it?

(a) The Council's hands are tied by the government.
(b) The Council can only do what government funds allow it to do.

Give a reason why the Arts Council spokeswoman used (a) rather than (b).

More than just words

• speculative basis	• on the basis of guesswork
• fundraising source of revenue	• income from fundraising

On the left are expressions used by the speaker (paragraph 3), and on the right possible alternatives. What impression does the speaker create about himself by his choice of words?

C Discussion

Do you think funding for the arts should come from public funds or from sponsorship? Do you think it important that people get a chance to see ballet? What qualities do you think a ballet dancer would need?

The voice of dance today

Ismene Brown talks to Peter Brinson, a combative dance guru who this week won the Digital Dance Award for 1992

Like footballers, dancers have an image problem. All legs, no brains, you might say; they need someone to do their thinking for them.

That is a judgement with which Dr Peter Brinson would not agree for a moment, but he would concede that dancers need someone to do their talking for them. And that explains how a first-class honours politics graduate from Oxford who saw ballet for the first time in his mid-twenties became chief spokesman for British dance.

This week Brinson was presented with the dance world's prestige prize for achievement, the Digital Dance Award for 1992, sponsored by the computer company. He won £30,000 for a dance venture of his choice, which will be the setting up of a pioneering dance injuries scheme.

Unglamorous but vital – which sums up his hugely influential backstage work in dance, abroad as well as here. In a sectarian dance world, where classical and contemporary dance scenes are hardly on speaking terms, he alone moves lightly among the factions.

He founded Ballet For All, the Royal Ballet's ballet-to-the-people wing; he was President of the Royal Academy of Dancing; he was for 10 years Director of the Gulbenkian Arts Foundation, which funds arts initiatives.

There are numerous Brinson books, reports, lectures, advisory chairs on major dance companies. All in all, people describe him as the guru of dance, the most powerful voice in dance today.

But it's a voice which has been known to upset people: inveighing against the Thatcherite values of the arts establishment, championing the downtrodden dance experimenters. Hence perhaps the tardiness of public recognition, which has arrived only in his mid-sixties.

After all, where are the problems? The Royal Ballet is holding up well. English National Ballet researchers report an increasing audience for ballet in general…

"When I talk about dance, I don't only think about classical dance. I think about contemporary dance, ballroom dancing, even folk dancing. As many people go to dance halls and discos as go to football. And I think one has to pay attention. Dance in general cultural thinking is right at the bottom of the heap."

Hence the three main wrongs that Brinson would like to see put right.

First, dance in state schools is short-changed by being classed as physical education, not as an art – turning it, he argues, into "a cul-de-sac". Next, children who want to take up dance training can get grants for only one specialist school, the Royal Ballet School. And finally, funding for dance companies – inadequate already – is biased towards mainstream work.

The fact that this is largely the result of historical prejudice is no excuse, argues Brinson. "There's no reason why the English can't develop a dance culture. In Tudor times we were known as 'the dancing English' and were famous for our galliard."

"The major killing field for dance was the 19th Century and the possession of our empire. This affected our whole education system. We had to breed a nation of colonial administrators, so physical education for boys was taken straight from the military manual."

Dr Brinson does not believe in only 'high art' – the lonely pursuit of excellence independent of society. "There's no chance of dance becoming a root, gutsy thing in British life unless the opportunities for dance at a community level are increased. And that means official support in education."

The Daily Telegraph – 10 October 1992

The voice of dance today

A Comprehension

1 List the biographical details that are given about Dr Brinson.

2 Give his understanding of the word 'dance', and say what reputation the English had in regard to dance in Tudor times.

B Language focus

Put it in your own words

Paraphrase Dr Brinson's comments in paragraph 11. Compare your version with the original and make a list of the linguistic changes you have made.

Fighting talk

The 'killing field' and the 'military manual' (paragraph 13): what changes in the national attitude towards the place of dance in English culture are expressed by the use of these terms?

The things he says...

Below are expressions used by Dr Brinson with possible alternatives. What does he want to say about dance that is best illustrated by his choice of words?

- at the bottom of the heap (paragraph 9)
  considered least important

- a root, gutsy thing (paragraph 14)
  a basic, passionate expression

Expressing it differently...

Below are alternative ways of saying the same thing:

(a) Dr Brinson would disagree with this judgement.
(b) Dr Brinson would not agree with this judgement.

What considerations would lead to the choice of one rather than the other?

C Discussion

What are your views on dance: should it form a vital part of a nation's cultural heritage? Can you think of any dances that are automatically associated with a particular country? What is your favourite form of dance? Do you prefer to watch dance, or to take part in it yourself?

Grand National preparations

Background

The Grand National is the most famous horse race in Britain and a national sporting event. Even people who do not normally watch racing watch the National because it is an exciting and often dramatic race. This is because it is a steeplechase, a race over jumps, and the course is so gruelling that often both horses and riders are badly injured. On the day well over 50,000 people attend the course, more than 15,000,000 British listeners and viewers tune in to the BBC coverage, and the world-wide television audience is estimated to be in excess of 750,000,000 people.

Pre-viewing

In this extract about a horse preparing for the Grand National you will meet the trainer, the jockey, and the vet.

1 Suggest a possible area of concern that they all share.

2 Make a note of three scenes you would expect to see in the video.

3 Do you think it is fair to expect the horse to risk injury or death in such a race?

Video

A The main issue

What unusual treatment did the horse receive?

Further details

1 What was the horse suffering from?

2 How did the horse respond to the treatment?

3 What are the advantages of this type of treatment?

4 What is Jenny Pitman's son, Mark, trying to do?

B Language focus

Different styles of writing...

A popular racing magazine wants a report of between seventy to eighty words on the treatment, from both the vet and the owner. Split into two groups; one group writing from the vet's point of view and being very factual and impersonal, and the other from the enthusiastic owner's point of view.

Afterwards, form pairs, with one coming from each group, and compare your different reports. Look at the style and the content, and discuss such things as sentence length, use of adjectives and the choice of vocabulary.

Saying it another way...

Keeping the meaning the same, rewrite the following sentences using the word in brackets:

e.g.There are no drugs in operation. (used) becomes No drugs are used. *or* There are no drugs used.

(a) Garrison Savannah is said to be a strong horse. (say)
(b) As a last resort he was given acupuncture. (they)

Answer the questions on the pairs of rewritten sentences that follow:

(i) Seeing him after his treatment I couldn't believe it. (when)
(ii) When I saw him after his treatment I couldn't believe it.

Suggest why the first rather than the second was used by the speaker in the television report.

(i) We're trying to even out the energy flow. (what)
(ii) What we're trying to do is even out the energy flow.

What effect does the vet achieve by using (ii) rather than (i)?

Putting words in their mouth

Below is a list of expressions used in the television report with a list of synonyms or near synonyms next to them. Say which ones would be appropriate for use in the contexts which follow them:

• from the horse's mouth	from a trustworthy source
• the scope is enormous	there is a wide variety of application
• the sky's the limit	the possibilities are endless

(a) a report written by a doctor about the uses of a new drug
(b) a conversation between friends with one trying to convince the other that the information he has comes from a reliable source
(c) a lecture by an engineer about the potential of a new invention
(d) an informal chat between colleagues about the future prospects of their very successful business

How can you tell?

Paragraph 9 of the transcript gives the jockey's views about the horse. Pick out two linguistic clues that would tell you that his views were originally spoken to someone rather than written down.

C Role play

Work in pairs, with one interviewing the other for the job of stable lad. From the information given in the video clip about the duties involved, discuss such things as likes and dislikes about certain aspects of the work, the qualities needed by someone working with horses, the unsociable hours of the job, and anything else you consider relevant.

Five-stroke rule will devalue the art of riding

Talking Racing – **Peter Scudamore**

From a jockey's point of view the issue of the whip is pretty distressing. There are many people – animal lovers, trainers, former jockeys and members of the press – who like to portray jockeys as butchers who ride with the sole intention of winning the race at whatever cost to the horse.

Nothing could be further from the truth. We are, however, caught in a dilemma because we believe that the correct use of the whip will make most horses at least maintain their maximum effort – if not in some cases actually go faster. Yet using the stick does at times cause limited damage to a horse.

Jockeys are just as concerned with the welfare of horses as the people who attack us. We are told jockeys in the past did not hit horses as hard, or as often, as modern ones. But when I looked after horses for my father as a lad, they sometimes came home with weals on them, just as they do now, and they were sometimes hit more than 10 times, which is today's limits.

My father rode for many years for Willie Stephenson – trainer of Derby and Grand National horses – who hated to see his horses hit too often. When a horse came in from a race, he would check to see if it was marked.

There were trainers who, occasionally, asked for their horse to be hit if needed. Nothing is different today. Some owners and trainers do not like to see their horses hit, but others believe a lazy horse should receive a reminder.

Unfortunately, I am serving the last day of a four-day suspension for marking a horse at Taunton. I did not hit him excessively, nor with any more force than I have hit any other horse this season. There is no doubt in my mind that without using the whip as I did, I would not have won the race. I have to go out and ride every horse better than my rivals. If I do not do so consistently, Martin Pipe could employ another jockey.

The stewards can fine and suspend me, but they do not employ me. If I do not please the owner and the trainer, I would not be on the horse in the first place.

The incident that cost me a suspension was in a small race at Taunton. Yet Adrian Maguire showed in last year's Gold Cup that the guidelines on using the stick go out of the window in a big race.

Following the Cheltenham showpiece, the stewards had little option but to suspend Maguire for four days, since he was found to have hit Cool Ground 20 times from the second last fence.

Yet had he not done so, the horse would not have won – a fact which lends credence to jockeys thinking that the stick makes a horse go faster.

Jockeys are being driven into a corner to defend the correct use of the stick because some employees of the Jockey Club look upon us as butchers, thus creating a wedge between the two parties instead of solving the problem. It has caused further discontent and is damaging to the interests of racing.

The Jockey Club brought in the 10-stroke whip guideline, which I believe to be good, as it has improved the standard of riding. However, the Jockey Club meet next Monday to discuss reducing this to five strokes, because of pressure mainly from the RSPCA. This is nonsense. It will devalue the art of riding.

It is the whip itself that is wrong. Although there are rules on the length and the width of the stick, the material it is made from is more important.

I know the Jockey Club are looking into this. Felt-covered sticks are often used but they are not the answer, because when it rains the felt soaks up the moisture and the stick can be more, not less, severe than the conventional one.

If a lightweight stick could be produced that would encourage a horse to maintain its effort without hurting or damaging it, all the parties would then be united in the best interests of racing.

We jockeys could then concentrate on getting the best out of our horses.

The Daily Telegraph – 2 February

Five-stroke rule will devalue the art of riding

A The main issue

1 Summarize the pros and cons of using the whip.

2 List the groups of people involved in the controversy.

Sorting out the details

1 Summarize the effects of the controversy on the jockeys.

2 State the writer's views on the 10-stroke guideline.

3 Explain the real problem with the whip.

B Language focus

From the animal lover's point of view...

The word 'butchers' is used twice in the article (paragraph 1 and paragraph 11) to describe the behaviour of the jockeys. What sort of images does this word convey? What is implied by its use?

Making it sound better than it is

Some owners and trainers think lazy horses should 'receive a reminder' (paragraph 5). What do they mean by this? Suggest a phrase an animal lover might use.

The jockey refers to 'limited damage' (paragraph 2). Do you think the RSPCA would be happy with this as a description of what happens to a horse when the whip is used? What might be their choice of words?

What did it say in the article?

Pick out the words or phrases in the article that mean the same as the following expressions:

(a) to be disregarded (paragraph 8)
(b) leads people to believe that something is true (paragraph 10)
(c) being put in a difficult or embarrassing position (paragraph 11)
(d) causing something to come between people or groups, and separate them (paragraph 11)
(e) to be investigating something (paragraph 14)

Why do you think the author preferred not to use (a) and (c) above?

What is he really saying?

The writer tells us that the stewards can fine and suspend him, but that they do not employ him (paragraph 7). Think about who does employ him, and why he is employed, and state what he is saying about the realities of his position as a jockey in a highly competitive sport.

C Saying your piece

Divide yourselves into three groups to represent the points of view of the jockeys, the Jockey Club, and the Royal Society for the Prevention of Cruelty to Animals (RSPCA). After spending a few minutes discussing the issue, each group is to choose a spokesperson to present its views to the other groups, leading to a question and answer session on the issues.

British Studies: horse-racing and other sports

National Opinion Poll Market Research conducted a survey in 1991 for the Race Course Association with the purpose of providing data that would help the RCA plan strategies for increasing the popularity of racegoing. In the first two paragraphs below are some of the facts and figures resulting from their survey.

Horse-racing and other sports

1 The following proportions have paid a visit to each of the sporting events surveyed:

Football	38%	Cricket	16%
Horse-racing	20%	Rugby	11%
Motor sport	18%	Golf	5%

Women form a large proportion of horse-racing attenders and potential attenders than any of the other sports: 44% of those who have ever visited horse-racing are women (compared to about 30% for all of the other sports).

Younger persons (fifteen to thirty-four) form a smaller proportion of the horse-racing audience than the other sports: 25% of those who have ever visited horse-racing are fifteen to thirty-four years old (compared to 45% for motor sport, for example).

2 Men are more likely to watch horse-racing on television (48% in the past year), but 38% of women have also watched it at some time in the past year.

The Race Course Association 1991

3 A successful day at the races consists of more than just watching the racing. Below is a list of various factors which contribute towards customer satisfaction:

(a) helpfulness of the staff
(b) good facilities for viewing the racing
(c) good catering facilities with a wide range of food and drink
(d) provision for entertaining young children
(e) good toilet facilities – clean toilets and enough of them to avoid long queues

Over to you

In the classroom

1 Are there any sports or sporting activities that are associated with a particular social class?

2 Suggest reasons why, although more women than men attend horse-racing, fewer of them watch it on television.

3 Give reasons why people would watch sport on television rather than attend it in person. Can you think of any sports that have been particularly popularized by television coverage?

Outside projects

1 Try to identify any sports or sporting activities in your country that are especially popular with:

(a) young people
(b) women

Make a list of them and suggest reasons for their popularity.

2 Each member of the group is to question six friends of under twenty-five years of age who have recently attended a sporting event, to find out the level of customer satisfaction. Compose a list of six items you all consider important, two of which must be different from those listed above, and produce your own set of statistics from the answers you receive, e.g. 25% were satisfied with the car-parking facilities. List the areas in which improvements could be made.

Flower thieves

Duration: 3 minutes and 3 seconds

Conservationists are worried that highly organized thieves could wipe out some species of Britain's rarest wild flowers. Rare plants and seeds are being stolen to meet an increasing need from gardeners and collectors. In Oxfordshire, volunteers are keeping a twenty-four hour guard on a field of rare orchids. They want tougher laws to protect the region's countryside. *Chris Bishop* reports.

In Oxfordshire's Chiltern Hills they're on the alert. People here are trying to protect one of Britain's rarest wild flowers. The monkey orchid, so called because of its shape, once carpeted the fields of southern England, but after years of ploughing and picking there are just two small patches left, in the Chilterns and south-east Kent. They're protected by law, and a £2,000 fine for damaging them, but their dwindling numbers are still under constant attack from rabbits, collectors, and thieves. Conservationists are paying these wardens to stop people stealing the last of the orchids, but in two months time the money runs out and these rare plants could be at the mercy of thieves.

I presume it's either motivated by greed because they think they can make money by selling these plants which they then find out they can't, or it's some sort of obsessive collecting notion they have; they just want to possess a rare British orchid. It all seems clearly pointless to me.

And what damage is it doing?

If you steal the flowering plant, the seeds are then not set. We don't get new plants coming in and the whole population just goes down.

It's not just the rare plants that are under attack. At this nature reserve in Surrey, conservationists are running patrols to protect more common wild flowers like bluebells and cowslips. They believe organized crime is plundering the nature reserves for wild flower plants and seeds. Recently, thirty acres of wild flowers here were stripped of seeds in a morning, setting back their spread.

There are gangs going out doing it early in the morning before the normal population gets up and takes their dogs for a walk and so on. And these gangs, what they must be doing is growing them on, growing them on to small plants and then selling them to nurseries and so on and so forth. Not the large reputable garden centres, but smaller, backstreet nurseries and so on. And these types of plants can sell £1.00, £1.50, £2.00 a time.

There seems to be a ready market for the pickings. Six bags of this sphagnum moss were seized before thieves had a chance to take it away for sale. It would have fetched around £400.00. One of the ironies of the situation is that the green revolution has made wild flower gardens very fashionable, so many of the people who claim to care for the countryside could indirectly be helping to destroy it. Conservationists are pressing, during National Environment Week for tighter laws. Among other changes, they want a ban on the taking of seeds, which is still legal. They fear otherwise, the organized thefts will increase, creating even more endangered species like the south-east's dwindling monkey orchid.

Salmon return to the Thames

Duration: 2 minutes and 16 seconds

The king of freshwater fish, the salmon, continues its slow but steady return to the waters of the Thames. Centuries ago they were abundant, but pollution drove them away from their ancestral spawning grounds. Today, the fish received a helping hand from the National Rivers Authority with the opening of two new salmon ladders to help the fish overcome man-made obstacles in the Surrey stretch of the river. But while many are claiming that the return of the Thames salmon is a sure sign that the battle against pollution is being won, some environmentalists remain unconvinced. *Shireen Wheeler* reports.

The National Rivers Authority is banking on salmon to clean up their image. More than a million of the young salmon smolts have been released into the Thames since the programme began to promote their population in 1979. These fish will swim out to sea, some returning as adults, hopefully to spawn. But many are becoming trapped in weirs as they make their way up the river. The NRA has planned twenty-two special salmon ladders to help them along the Thames. Two of these were opened at Chertsey and Sunbury today.

Salmon are regarded by a lot of people as a very important monitor of water quality. They have very strict requirements in terms of dissolved oxygen levels and also river temperature and fresh water flow. They have strict requirements, and if those requirements aren't met, then the salmon aren't going to be able to navigate – well, it could be the most precarious part of the river, which is the tideway.

Two hundred years ago this river was full of salmon. But by 1834, their home had become so polluted that the species completely died out. And then, in 1974, some stray salmon were sighted. The then keepers of the river, Thames Water, seized on this as proof of the success of their clean-up policies. But environmentalists are not so sure.

We mustn't allow ourselves to be blinded to the fact that, the salmon being present in the river is an indication of improvement, but it's also an indication of perhaps how much more we have to do. The animals don't yet breed in the Thames, and they don't go through their full life-cycle there. It's really at this stage, a cosmetic exercise.

But the final proof of how successful the NRA's programme has been, will be seen in how many of the adult fish return and stay to breed.

Cardiac patients and relatives

Duration: 2 minutes and 28 seconds

A heart transplant programme at Harefield Hospital in Middlesex is experiencing serious problems providing accommodation for the families of patients. Doctors encourage relations to stay with cardiac patients especially children, but some people are being forced to sleep in caravans or on hospital floors to be near their loved ones. *Stephanie McNair* reports.

Five-and-a-half year-old John Carr lives in Lanarkshire. Four weeks ago he had a heart transplant. His parents have left their home and their two-year-old son in Scotland and they're having to stay in a caravan in the grounds of Harefield Hospital to be near their son. Ten days ago, the one they'd been lent by a friend was stolen along with £1,000 worth of money and clothes. This is a replacement from a well-wisher. But on most nights Margaret Carr has to sleep on the floor of John's room because he gets frightened. In spite of the problems, they're convinced they should be with John.

It's part of John getting better. But as a mother I couldn't possibly be in Scotland 400 miles away and with John down here, despite the fact that the nurses are very good. So we need to be here, we need to be together.

Are you surprised that the hospital isn't able to provide you with any more permanent accommodation?

Not really because I think hospitals don't have the kind of money to provide this type of accommodation and so the funding has to come from somewhere, and it's sad that the money isn't there to provide it. I don't know that people are aware of the need, perhaps that's the problem.

Harefield now does two hundred heart operations a year, including transplants. Doctors believe the patient's close family play a crucial role in their recovery.

Obviously we want them to feel as secure as possible. They're going through very stressful times being in hospital, a lot of strangers, so the more things that they have that make them feel secure and comfortable and everything else, and siblings have a very important role to play in that. Obviously the other thing is that the siblings themselves suffer. I mean the patient isn't the only one that suffers when a child's going through all of this. Parents suffer, the patient suffers, and the siblings, so if you can keep them all together, then it helps.

Harefield needs accommodation for at least fifty families. It can only just cater for thirty, sometimes for up to three months at a time. Staff are now so concerned they're planning to start an appeal to build more rooms.

We can't always provide accommodation for both parents so often we have the mother here and the father's left at home. We have no accommodation for any siblings at all so the family's invariably split. Obviously it adds enormously to their stress.

The appeal which is still being set up would need to raise two million pounds to provide enough room for just eight families.

Lasers in dentistry

Duration: 2 minutes and 22 seconds

For many people, a visit to the dentist can be a traumatic experience. But a Kent dentist has just taken delivery of a revolutionary laser which may do away with the need for drilling, injections, and even pain. Sounds almost too good to be true. *Robin Gibson* has been finding out more.

A visit to the dentist even today, however accomplished the chairside manner, it can cut even the steeliest nerve down to size. It's estimated that only about thirty per cent of people in Britain visit their dentist regularly. Many of those who don't are put off by the drill, or the needle. So dentists welcome anything which can make their life easier, and that's where this new dental laser comes in. The handful of dentists who have this new technology are proclaiming a revolution. It can be used to numb teeth, replacing the injection, and to vaporize decay in place of the drill.

People, when they come to me, are always very, very nervous, and it's mainly about the injection, and the pain from the drills. Now this laser, because it vaporizes the decay with light pulses, we now don't need to use the slow speed drill, so it cuts out all the vibration as a thing of the past. It's quite noisy, but there shouldn't be any pain at all. Quite a dramatic sight. Now the actual light beam is now creating a hole in your tooth as it vaporizes the decay.

The American-made laser is as yet some way from being sufficiently developed to replace drills and needles completely, but there have been some impressive spin-off effects, such as the treatment of mouth ulcers and sensitive teeth.

It's not as sensitive as it was is it?

No.

OK, now that means that it's actually gradually desensitizing the tooth now.

The high cost of the equipment, £35,000, means dentists will be charging for its use, but in his surgery at Staplehurst in Kent, Peter Garrod is planning to make it available to National Health patients. The cost – £30.00 a filling.

Indian pupils come top

Duration: 2 minutes and 30 seconds

A new survey has found that pupils of Indian origin are coming top of the class, and it concludes that parents should copy the Indian example of setting goals and offering more support. In its widest-ever survey the Inner London Education Authority studied the results of twenty thousand pupils and found English, Welsh and Scots children did badly compared to those of Asian background. The details from *Steven Gardner*.

This final end-of-term report commissioned by ILEA's research unit concludes that race and social class are still the two most dominant factors in determining examination results. Based on the exam results of sixteen-year-olds throughout the capital, the survey says that Indian children from predominantly middle-class backgrounds scored the best results, whilst those from the more socially deprived Bangladeshi, Caribbean and Turkish communities performed significantly less well. The survey also found that while Church of England schools did no better than county schools, students at Roman Catholic schools, where there was evidence of strong teacher and parental involvement, did better. While the survey stresses that ILEA's policies have already led to increased achievement levels, it says continued improvement will depend on greater parental and teacher expectations coupled with improved students' self-esteem.

The lesson to pass on to the boroughs is one that they should pass on to the government: they will need far more money to improve performance, to motivate teachers, to see that the pupils have got the materials that they need to learn more, and that they get the extra help and support that the poorest city in the whole country needs, in order to provide the standards of education and reach the levels of attainment that parents living in London are entitled to expect for their children.

One of the messages it has for schools is the need for them to work more closely with the parents to raise the parents' expectations. Very often you see, it will be not that the parents don't want their children to do well but that they don't know themselves what their children are capable of achieving, or what the school system is capable of providing for them, and so the schools have an educational job to do with the parents as well as with the children.

Although today's survey is definitely the last to be produced under the auspices of the Inner London Education Authority, as far as its Central Research Unit is concerned, that's been given a last minute reprieve. In a special deal between ILEA and the London School of Economics, in future the Unit will be housed at the London College in order that it can continue to monitor the educational performance of the capital.

Teacher stress

Duration: 2 minutes and 36 seconds

A report out today says rowdy pupils and aggressive parents are causing serious mental and physical problems among teachers. The Health and Safety Commission says millions of pounds is lost each year because teachers can't cope with the increasing stress. This report from *Alison Holt*.

The report claims that life in the classroom is leaving teachers as casualties. The numerous education changes in recent years coupled with aggressive pupils and parents, are blamed for a sharp increase in the pressures teachers face, leaving many unable to cope. It's something the profession has warned of. This east London office of the National Union of Teachers offers counselling for the many who ring for help.

One of the tragedies of the situation is that we don't hear about the problems until they've gone really too far, when we're talking about trying to assist members as best we can who are heading for nervous breakdowns.

Carole Shaw is one of those teachers who found the stress too much. She taught languages to eleven to sixteen-year-olds at an east London school, but a few months ago she resigned.

I had various physical complaints, and in the end I had to take more and more time off work. I think that there are just too many changes happening too fast, too many demands being made of people which I don't think are humanly achievable. I just don't think you can pay attention to them all and do justice to them.

The report estimates ten per cent of teachers become seriously mentally or physically ill because of stress, with another thirty per cent suffering from less serious illnesses. The result, the Commission says, is absenteeism, reduced productivity, and teachers leaving the profession. The financial cost, it claims, runs into millions of pounds. The report guidelines are being sent to head teachers and local authorities, outlining programmes they can run to cut classroom stress.

There's a lot, we think, that is to do with management, and we want to make stress a management issue. We want to waken up management at all levels to facing up to problems of stress.

We think the government needs to look at the pace of the changes it's implementing. We think that teachers need to be involved in the design of change at all levels, whether it's national level through their representatives in unions, or local authority level or school level. And we think the government does need to look at the grotesque under-funding of the education service.

The Department of Education says it can't comment on the report directly as it hasn't seen it yet, but it says that teaching has always been a stressful and challenging profession, and that the short-term increased work-load for teachers will have long-term benefits for education.

Problems of the elderly

Duration: 2 minutes and 29 seconds

More and more elderly people seem destined to live out their days neglected and alone. According to new research published today, the caring professions are struggling to keep pace with the increase in the numbers of old people. But the elderly can be surprisingly resilient. *Sue Bishop's* been to meet one woman celebrating her hundredth birthday today, cheerfully enduring a Dickensian life-style at Kingston in Surrey.

Bertha Taylor is one of those old ladies about whom everyone says, 'Isn't she marvellous' and she's just that. Every day she slowly, painstakingly dresses herself with help from her devoted eighty-four-year-old sister-in-law, Lily. She has to sleep in the front room, because she can no longer manage the stairs, but Bertha, Bertie to her family, is tougher than she looks. Today is her hundredth birthday, and she begins it like every day since she moved here in 1896 with a wash under a cold tap. It's the only water supply. She goes to the garden to go to the loo and to the kettle to get hot water.

I don't notice it, dear. John, my nephew, wanted to have some water laid on but I wouldn't have ... I didn't want it. I said, Oh, I liked it as it is.

Do you mind having an outside loo?

No, not at all. Because I can get out there with the help of somebody if they take me. I'm quite all right. I don't feel any different except that it's my legs. I can't walk. If I could only walk.

Today Bertha celebrates more than her hundredth birthday; it's a victory against the adversities of old age. It's fitting that it's also the day the Family Policy Studies Centre has chosen to publish its report *Community care and elderly people*. In it, they warn of a widening gap in service provision for women like Bertha. They say they're being abandoned to fend for themselves. By 2001 the number of people over eighty-five in Britain will be more than a million, over double the 1981 figure. Now many, like Bertha, have no home help, no meals on wheels, just a wheelchair.

What I get is my pension, and Lily gets £25.00 a week for looking after me, from the Social Security.

Do you get any other help?

No other help.

But as Bertha goes for her birthday jaunt to the outside privy, she knows others endure much greater hardships.

Everybody hasn't got someone as good as Lily to look after them, have they? I'm one of the lucky ones.

Job cuts at the Natural History Museum

Duration: 2 minutes and 9 seconds

More than three hundred staff at the Natural History Museum have been holding a one-day strike in protest at plans to cut jobs. One hundred posts are likely to go as part of a radical reorganization of the Museum, the largest of its kind in the world. *Duncan Kennedy* reports.

The Natural History Museum's first official strike in its 109 years has all the unacademic antics of any other industrial dispute: picket lines, banners, and disgruntled workers. In this case the issue is the loss of one hundred scientific, technical and administrative jobs. Staff say the cuts at a museum which attracts one-and-three-quarter million visitors a year are unacceptable.

Well what the Director seems to be saying is he'll get rid of our long-term staff, who've spent their lives here, and buy in short-term staff who'll maybe come for a couple of years. He was talking about new blood. But that shows he doesn't understand the kind of science this museum's for. Because we are a world centre in a very unique kind of science.

This chap's a diplodocus from the Isle of Wight actually.

It says Wyoming, Leslie.

Wyoming. Right.

The job cuts come at a time when the Museum is doing all it can to sell itself in a cultural climate underpinned by economic stringency. The target of the picketers' protest is the Museum's director, Dr Neil Chalmers, the man who took over in 1988 to take on the Museum's giant problems.

They're going for two reasons, these posts. First, frankly we do not have the money that we need to run the Museum at the size it is at present. Secondly, we do need to make some changes in the Museum, to make us stronger in some areas, to concentrate our scientific research into certain areas, and so we need to restructure the Museum.

Dr Chalmers says he can't rule out more job losses if funds get tighter still. Sponsorship, he says, is now the name of the game, with BP alone pumping in a million pounds. He says the jobs must go to provide more flexibility in a streamlined museum. The Museum itself remains open throughout all the wrangling, with those whose jobs are now under threat at this museum of natural history, increasingly concerned about the future.

Heathrow runways

Duration: 3 minutes

British Midland Airways have called for more planes to be allowed to use Heathrow airport. They've suggested a package of measures which would mean that another 200 aircraft will be able to take off or land every day. But there's been a furious reaction from people who live near the airport who say it would mean even more noise and disruption. *Brian Milligan* reports.

With passenger numbers expected to double between now and the year 2000, Britain is already chronically short of airport capacity. Despite the possibility of a fifth terminal, Heathrow will run out of space next year, and the experts agree a new runway would be needed somewhere in the south-east within a decade. In the meantime, British Midland say capacity at Heathrow could be increased by ten per cent with what they call mixed mode operation. At present the airport has two parallel runways. In the morning, aeroplanes will land on one of them, and take off on the other, giving residents in Longford and Hatton some respite from the noise. After 3 o'clock in the afternoon the situation is reversed, so those living in Cranford and Stanwell Moor get a bit of a rest. With mixed mode operation, both runways would be used for take-offs and landings, meaning all areas would be subject to constant daytime noise. This method is already used at Gatwick with its single runway, and in the States, and it's said to be no more dangerous than the existing system.

Heathrow is a vital national asset. It is a hub airport for Britain and if we don't develop Heathrow vigorously and allow it to rise to its full potential, the traffic will simply be taken away, not to other British airports but it will fly from Brussels or Amsterdam or Paris.

British Midland also want to increase capacity by cutting down on the interval between planes, and by lengthening the working day by an hour. All this meets with heavy local opposition.

We'll certainly go to the Minister and say that he really should not consider this, inflicting this on the people round Heathrow. They really do have enough to put up with already.

And Michael Rayner has more to put up with than most. He's taken his fight against aircraft noise to the European Court of Human Rights, for the farm he runs near Colnbrook is directly under the flight-path of Heathrow's northern runway. If British Midland get their way, he'll no longer get half a day's respite from the worst of the noise.

It would affect our lives very seriously, and certainly something that I would want to fight very hard to prevent happening.

Today MPs from the Heathrow area met up to organize opposition to the British Midland proposals, and to ask the CAA to ignore them.

My constituents in Stanwell organize their day by that 3 o'clock switch. If they've got to go shopping, to visit friends, they do it at the noisy time of day, and do their gardening and sit at home when it's quiet, and I'm blowed if I'm going to allow the profits of British Midland to be put before the sort of peace of mind of the residents of Stanwell.

In the meantime, the Department of Transport is actively looking at the proposals but won't comment further. In the context of the 1990s, the government can't afford to ignore ideas like this; it's also a long way from giving them the go-ahead.

Villagers and speeding traffic

Duration: 2 minutes and 2 seconds

And now, another kind of road problem. Motorists speeding through an Essex village have been shocked to find residents pointing a gun at them. People living at Theydon Bois near Epping are so fed up with road-hogs that they have bought their own police-style speed gun to collect evidence about the number of people breaking the law. *Rebecca Garrat* reports.

It's hard to tell you're only a couple of miles from the M 25, until you see the traffic. Every rush hour, hundreds of cars and lorries thunder down this little road, travelling up to twice the 30 mile-an-hour speed limit. It's been a constant worry for the residents.

It does go through your mind every time you cross the road, this could be the last time. We've had a lot of problems with the speeding motorists. We have vehicles mounting the pavement, causing people to scatter to escape injury. We've had the noise of speeding vehicles. When the Council came to have a look at the situation, the Epping Forest District Council representative told us not to confuse noise with speed. So we realized we had to find a way to actually prove, to them, that vehicles were speeding.

The money for the speed gun was raised in less than a week. Residents spent hours clocking the vehicles and amassing data so they could prove to the Council that there was a case for changing the road, but the Council say they have other priorities.

We've got 2,000 places within Essex where we've got a worse accident record. Now it is surely right that we deal with the places where people are actually being injured, rather than where they might be, regrettable though that may be.

The police say they haven't the resources to monitor the traffic all the time, but the residents won't give up.

We've tried the police, we've tried the Local Authority. We really think we've tried everything we can, except for taking legal action against the Local Authority.

In the meantime, the locals' only hope is that drivers slow down voluntarily, before tragedy strikes on the B 172.

Women priests

Duration: 2 minutes and 13 seconds

As the Church of England begins the process of voting on whether to accept women priests, clergy in the diocese of Rochester in Kent will tomorrow be among the first in the south-east to make up their minds. As *Amanda Harper* reports, feelings are already running high.

The ancient city of Rochester, flanked by the River Medway and guarded by its castle. Here for the last 1,400 years, people have worshipped at the Cathedral. But tomorrow, a wider and more controversial issue, the ordination of women into the priesthood, will be discussed. Rochester is the first diocese in the south-east to vote on the issue. For Reverend Judith Rose, Chaplain to the Bishop of Rochester, the choice is clear. As a deacon she can carry out many responsibilities, but she's unable to hold Communion or run her own church, because she's not an ordained priest.

I would see the priesthood as, not only representing Christ to embrace the whole of humanity, not just maleness, but also representing the People of God, and that's made up of men and women. And so I think we would have a much more representative priesthood if it had women as well as men, so women can bring their distinctive contribution alongside the men.

I don't believe that leadership in the Church is reserved for the male. But there are those who firm..., who honestly believe that it is, really based on the fact that Christ was a male, and that He chose twelve apostles who were all male. My argument would be that was in first century society, and that things have changed a good deal since then.

While there's a large number of people in the diocese in favour of women priests, those against their ordination are just as vehement.

I think for the Church of England at the present time, it would be divisive within the Church, and I think it would also cut us off from the great Churches of Orthodoxy and Roman Catholicism which we've always claimed to be joined on to, rather like a branch of the tree. And what I see the General Synod doing at the moment is sitting on the branch with a saw, you know, about to saw off the branch that we're sitting on.

It's thought that Rochester will vote in favour of women priests. But even if it does, the matter still has to be discussed by the General Synod, and then a decision won't be expected until 1994.

Christ and Christmas

Duration: 2 minutes and 39 seconds

With just thirty-three shopping days to go until Christmas, new research has revealed that two-thirds of the population think that it's become too commercial. The poll coincides with the start of a campaign in over two-and-a-half thousand churches around the country to put Christ back into Christmas. *Alison Holt* reports.

Only another thirty-three shopping days to Christmas, and the drive to get us to buy more toys, more food, more everything, is well under way. But this Christmas, churches of all denominations are on the offensive. Their campaign 'Christmas Unwrapped', aims to remind us what Christmas is meant to be about. Peter Corson is a Baptist minister in Streatham in south London. He's one of the many ministers involved in the campaign.

The birth of Jesus was, from a Christian point of view, a world-changing happening, but most people now actually spend Christmas thinking primarily of themselves and what they can get, not necessarily what they can give.

He believes too many people have forgotten that December 25th is celebrating Christ's birth.

How do you feel about the thought that Christmas is actually the birthday of Jesus? I mean, do you think you tend to forget it as people in general ...

I think, yes, I'm sure the little ones don't think about it at all.

What is important to you about Christmas?

Presents really. I don't go to church or anything like that.

You know, they say a little baby was born in a manger so many years ago, but that's a story. Whether you believe it or not, that's up to you.

The survey carried out for 'Christmas Unwrapped' reveals there's room for change. Sixty per cent of people surveyed said they were unhappy with the way advertisers exploit Christmas; thirty-five per cent believed the exploitation needs to be cut out of the celebrations. But perhaps more worrying for the churches, forty-two per cent said it wouldn't affect their Christmas at all if there was no mention of the Nativity. The churches have decided to fight that with all the weapons of the hard-sell advertising campaign.

Our task this Christmas as Christians is simply to present our culture with this Jesus. Not as a fairy-tale fiction story who goes along with Peter Pan, and the Tooth Fairy, but to present Him in His reality ...

That reality will mean a poster campaign and video, as well as a series of concerts and carol services. In addition, there'll be 300 'Christmas Cracker' restaurants where you pay more and eat less for charity. All to get us to think again about Christmas.

Blind people and art

Duration: 2 minutes and 57 seconds

Arts lovers who happen to be blind or partially sighted are being given a new way of enjoying paintings and sculpture. The Tate Gallery in London is using specially constructed copies of famous paintings to help the blind feel the wonders of art. *Paul Anstiss* reports.

Carolyn James from Twickenham has been totally blind for twenty-six years. She loves art and often paints, drawing from memory the colours and shapes she once saw. But only now has she ventured back to a public art gallery to once again see the works of great masters, this time through her fingertips.

You should be able to trace the outline of this platform starting at the left-hand edge of the thermoform by the broken-off shoulder of the statue, and continuing on its other side.

The Tate Gallery, in collaboration with the Living Paintings Trust, has produced an album consisting of tapes and low relief diagrams that map out famous paintings for visually impaired people.

Most blind people have seen at some time or other, and I couldn't remember what certain paintings looked like, what sculptures looked like, or anything like that at all. So when the thermoforms came along and they said, 'Carolyn, have a feel', you know, I was ecstatic because it was like sort of going back to square one, starting all over again, and here was a door opening whereas normally all the doors closed like crazy.

Paintings like Picasso's *Nude woman in a red armchair* have been transformed into plastic images called thermoforms. Peter Fowler is one of the artists involved in the project. Interpreting works such as Caravaggio's *Supper at Emmaus* which has a lot of shadows can be difficult.

In reality a shadow is intangible, and the blind person doesn't usually feel a shadow, so of course in that case I used a texture to represent the shadow as a symbol really.

Modern works can be just as problematic.

For instance, in this one by Richard Hamilton where he's created this very strong illusion here, and then able to just hint at it and create an ambiguous form up here, in the original that I made, when I made this big form, it's not so easy in reality to lose it in this way.

There are three albums containing ten paintings each. Plastic sheeting is heated to make it pliable, a vacuum then sucks out the image to create the thermoform.

We wanted to choose works which would make a good map, that had very strong forms, which this one does. And we also thought ... this one in particular I think is one of our most marvellous early modern pictures.

Blind people can also see by touch, some of the Tate's pieces of sculpture. By prior arrangement a guide will take individuals through a whole new world including that of Picasso.

London ballet company to close

Duration: 1 minute and 59 seconds

The London City Ballet, which has the Princess of Wales as patron said today that it will have to shut down because it's run out of money. The company say that, in spite of success at the box-office, the show won't go on after June unless the Arts Council comes to the rescue. *Paul Anstiss* reports.

Box-office receipts at the London City Ballet have never been better. Average audiences regularly fill eighty-five per cent of capacity and bring in £700,000 a year. Business sponsorship raises another £500,000, but that still leaves a shortfall of half a million pounds towards the company's annual cost of £1.7 million. The company says additional fundraising by patrons like the Princess of Wales can no longer be relied on to make up the difference.

This gap that's not met by fundraising is getting wider and wider, and we feel that as directors, we just cannot go forward on such a speculative basis, assuming that we can perform miracles and create this huge fundraising source of revenue on an ongoing basis.

This year the Arts Council gave the City Ballet £100,000 to perform in places where the company would not normally visit because it wouldn't be economical. Next year even that money will be cut to £89,000. What the thirteen-year-old ballet company is asking for is an annual grant in addition to that used to offset touring costs so that it can properly plan its future.

Well, we're a highly successful touring ballet company. We tour all over England, Scotland, Wales. I think that if the company folds there's going to be a huge gap left, and if the Arts Council then go and try and fund something new, it's going to cost them an awful lot more money.

A spokeswoman for the Arts Council said the Council's hands are tied by the government. She said if the company does close in June, it would be regrettable.

Grand National preparations

Duration: 2 minutes and 10 seconds

It's the Grand National on Saturday, and one of the most fancied runners is the Berkshire-trained Garrison Savannah, the winner of the Cheltenham Gold Cup. But according to his trainer, Jenny Pitman, the horse wouldn't have been fit to run at all this season without the help of ancient Chinese medicine and an Oxfordshire vet. *Chris Bishop* got the story from the horse's mouth.

Dawn, the thunder of hooves greets the day at Lambourn in Berkshire as Jenny Pitman's stables prepare for another Grand National. Garrison Savannah carries the hopes of this stable. The Cheltenham Gold Cup winner is second favourite, but he races only after an astounding comeback from injury. Garrison Savannah suffered from torn leg muscles. As a last resort he was given acupuncture, a treatment of needles and electricity to stimulate the body's healing powers.

Seeing the horse after his very first treatment, I couldn't believe it. It was just unbelievable. He walked out of his box and he was well stiff in his off fore-shoulder, and Mr Day put the needles in him, and by the time he walked back up the yard, which is probably fifty yards, he was a different horse.

Here, stablemate Eric's Train gets similar treatment.

What we're trying to do is to even out and harmonize the energy flow.

Acupuncture for race-horses has to be combined with traditional training to be successful. In racing circles it's seen as an experiment.

The scope is enormous. There are no drugs in operation, so there is no problem with residues or doping or anything like that. You're only stimulating the natural processes, so you know, the sky's the limit to what you're able to try and do, and there's no reason why its popularity shouldn't grow.

These stables produced the 1983 Grand National winner Corbière. Now it's up to Jenny Pitman's son, Mark, to try and bring home a second winner.

He's a nice horse to ride, he jumps very well, he listens to what I have to say to him which is always very nice you know, so all things being equal he ought to be great.

Garrison Savannah is said to be a strong, aggressive horse able to cope well with high fences. If it wins on Saturday it'll be the first Grand National and Gold Cup double winner for nearly sixty years.